Time-Traveling Historians!

Bringing the Past to Life with STEM

Beverly Simmons and Jeannie Ruiz

Printing Futures

Printing Futures
Publishing in the Great Northwest

Time-Traveling Historians!

ISBN-13: 978-1-942357-92-6

Paperback Version

Cover design by: KDP Book Cover Maker

Dedication

To my fellow educators—those I've taught beside, learned from, and shared the journey with.

I wrote the STEM Across the Curriculum: PD Reimagined Series because today's students are growing up in a world profoundly shaped by artificial intelligence—and we, as educators, deserve professional development that reflects the urgency and complexity of that reality.

This book is dedicated to all of you who have always done your best to prepare students not just for the tests of today, but for the challenges of tomorrow.

"Are you ready to bring STEM out of the room down the hall and into every classroom—making it an integrated, empowering experience for every student?"

TABLE OF CONTENTS

"Are you ready to bring STEM out of the room down the hall and into every classroom—making it an integrated, empowering experience for every student?"

STEM-Integrated Social Studies & History Lesson Plans

Each lesson is introduced with a Story!

Time-Traveling Historians!
Bringing the Past to Life with STEM

STEM-Integrated Social Studies & History Lesson Plans

3. Factory Data: Industrialization and Urban Growth (page 35)

- **Topic:** U.S. or European Industrial Revolution
- **STEM Focus:** Graphing urban population shifts, pollution, factory output, labor conditions
- **Project:** Create a town plan based on industrial-era data and propose reforms

4. Voting Through the Decades (page 49)

- **Topic:** U.S. suffrage movements and voting trends
- **STEM Focus:** Analyze historical voter turnout data by race, gender, and region
- **Project:** Create an infographic that models how access and policies affected turnout

5. Mapping Empires and Resistance (page 63)

- **Topic:** European colonization and Indigenous resistance (world history)
- **STEM Focus:** Geographic information systems (GIS) mapping, demographic impact over time
- **Project:** Analyze population and territorial data to create before/after models

6. War, Technology, and Data: WWI (page 75)

- **Topic:** World War I military technology and human cost
- **STEM Focus:** Analyze casualty data, tech innovations (gas, trench warfare, tanks)
- **Project:** Model a new wartime tech and present its pros/cons using data visuals

7. Red Lines: Gerrymandering and Political Power (page 85)

- **Topic:** Representation and redistricting in the U.S.
- **STEM Focus:** Spatial data analysis, statistics in drawing district maps
- **Project:** Redraw a district map to reduce bias using population and voting data

STEM-Integrated Social Studies & History Lesson Plans

8. Climate and Conflict: The Dust Bowl (page 97)

- **Topic:** Environmental history of the 1930s
- **STEM Focus:** Analyze soil data, precipitation patterns, and migration maps
- **Project:** Build a soil conservation plan supported by graphed historical weather data

---

9. Propaganda, Media & Public Opinion (page 109)

- **Topic:** WWII propaganda or Cold War media
- **STEM Focus:** Quantify media reach, public sentiment surveys, tech in messaging
- **Project:** Run a classroom "media campaign" with measured reach and response

---

10. Rights in Real Time: Civil Rights and Public Policy (page 120)

- **Topic:** Civil Rights Movement in the U.S.
- **STEM Focus:** Use data from arrest records, marches, voter registration drives
- **Project:** Analyze impact and growth of activism with a visual data timeline

---

11. Trade Routes and Globalization

- **Topic:** Silk Road, Trans-Saharan trade, or modern global trade (page 136)
- **STEM Focus:** Create flow diagrams of traded goods, measure economic and cultural diffusion
- **Project:** Use real or historical trade data to simulate supply/demand across regions

---

12. Modern Policy Lab: Environmental Legislation (page 149)

- **Topic:** Modern U.S. or global environmental policies (Clean Air Act, Paris Agreement)
- **STEM Focus:** Graph CO_2 trends, analyze legislation outcomes, project future scenarios
- **Project:** Draft a student-led environmental policy with data to support its proposal

Art of STEM

Lesson 1: Mapping the Spread – The Columbian Exchange

📄 Marco and the Mystery of the Mango

An Introduction to the Columbian Exchange

Marco loved mangoes. Sweet, golden, juicy mangoes. Every Saturday, his family visited a farmers' market in the city, and Marco would run straight to the mango stand to pick the ripest one.

But one sunny Saturday, as he peeled back the fruit's skin, he paused and asked, "Where do mangoes even come from?"

His dad smiled. "That's a great question. To answer it, you have to go way back in time. All the way to a moment when the world changed forever—when two worlds met."

"Like a movie?" Marco asked.

"Exactly. A global adventure. It's called the Columbian Exchange."

Marco blinked. "Did it involve pirates?"

His dad laughed. "No pirates. But there were ships. Lots of them. In 1492, Christopher Columbus sailed from Europe and landed in the Americas. He thought he'd found a new route to Asia—but instead, he and others opened the door to a global exchange of plants, animals, people, ideas, and even diseases between Europe, Africa, and the Americas."

Marco listened as his dad described the ripple effect: Europeans brought horses, wheat, sugarcane, and cattle to the Americas. Native Americans introduced Europeans to potatoes, tomatoes, chocolate, corn, and yes—Marco's precious mangoes, which had journeyed from Asia to the Americas along new trade routes.

"But not everything traded was good," his dad said. "Diseases like smallpox were carried to the Americas, where Native communities had no immunity. Millions died."

Marco frowned. "So... they didn't just trade food?"

"No. They traded everything. Some of it helped people live longer, others brought suffering. But every trade had an effect. A cause and an effect. And every effect led to something else. Ecosystems changed. Diets changed. Cultures were forever transformed."

That night, Marco sat at the kitchen table and opened his school tablet. He zoomed in on a digital map of the Columbian Exchange—arrows showing corn heading to Europe, horses coming to the Americas, and oranges crossing the ocean.

He traced the path of the mango—South Asia to West Africa to South America. "So this fruit," he said, holding up the half-eaten mango, "has been on a bigger adventure than I have."

His dad smiled. "History is just a big map of connections, Marco. And the Columbian Exchange? It's one of the biggest connection stories in the world."

Marco took another bite of his mango and thought, *I'm going to learn everything I can about this exchange. Because every bite has a backstory.*

Discussion Questions

What surprised Marco about where mangoes came from?

What is the Columbian Exchange and why is it important?

Can you name three things that were traded across the world during the Columbian Exchange?

How did the Columbian Exchange affect the environment and people's lives?

Why is it important to understand cause and effect in history?

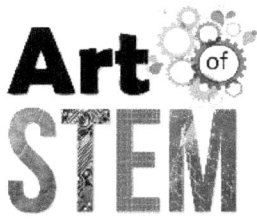

Lesson 1: Mapping the Spread – The Columbian Exchange

Topic: Biological and Cultural Exchange Post-1492

STEM Focus: Data mapping, systems thinking, environmental science

Subject Areas: World History, U.S. History, Geography, Environmental Studies

💬 Teacher Letter

Dear Educator,

This lesson is designed to support your efforts to teach historical content with depth while equipping students with valuable STEM skills—especially in data collection, interpretation, systems thinking, and visual modeling.

The Columbian Exchange provides a natural opportunity to examine cause and effect, the complexity of ecological and economic systems, and long-term human impact on the environment and culture. By introducing mapping tools and data analysis, students practice interpreting patterns and making evidence-based claims—essential skills in both history and science.

This 5E-format lesson supports interdisciplinary goals, encouraging students to think critically about the world as an interconnected system. While firmly grounded in social studies content, it models how STEM can be used as a lens to analyze, communicate, and deepen historical understanding.

This approach empowers your students to move beyond memorizing names and dates, and instead engage with history as active investigators—an experience that's both more rigorous and more rewarding.

Warm regards,
Beverly Simmons
Author, Educator, Curriculum Developer
STEMConnector's 100 Women Leaders in STEM
State Department International STEM Speaker

5E Lesson Plan: The Columbian Exchange

Adapt The Lesson to Your Schedule.

Engage

Activity:
Show students a basket or image containing bananas, potatoes, tomatoes, corn, and chocolate. Ask: *"Where do you think each of these foods originated?"* Then, reveal which were native to the Americas vs. Europe, Asia, or Africa.

Discussion Prompt:

- Why do you think these foods are so common today, even outside their region of origin?

Explore

Activity:
Students work in teams to research the origin and spread of key crops, animals, diseases, and technologies across continents after 1492.

Data Tool:
Provide a basic dataset (or link) showing:

- Where items originated
- When/where they spread
- Impact on population, diet, or environment

Task:
Plot item movement on a world map (digital or paper). Use arrows or icons to indicate direction and type (e.g., food, disease, animal).

Explain

Teacher-Guided Discussion:
Lead students in identifying patterns:

- Which regions gained/lost population?
- How did imported foods change diets and farming?
- What were the unintended consequences (e.g., invasive species, pandemics)?

Mini-Lecture or Reading:
Introduce the term "Columbian Exchange" and explain its significance using historical and ecological lenses.

Extend

Project Option:
Students choose one item (e.g., potatoes, smallpox, horses) and research its journey and impact using a cause-effect chain or infographic.

STEM Focus:
Encourage students to include data points, such as crop yield increases, population growth, and ecological impact, in their visuals.

Evaluate

Assessment Options:

- Exit ticket: Describe two long-term effects of the Columbian Exchange and how they're still seen today.
- Presentation rubric for project
- Peer map critiques based on accuracy, clarity, and reasoning

UNIT PLAN – Mapping the Spread in 4 DAYS

Mapping the Spread: The Columbian Exchange Unit Plan

Unit Duration: 4 School Days
Grade Level: Adaptable for Middle-High

Topic: Biological and Cultural Exchange Post-1492
STEM Focus: Data mapping, systems thinking, environmental science
Subject Areas: World History, U.S. History, Geography, Environmental Studies

---

Day 1: Introduction to the Columbian Exchange

Objective:
Students will understand the concept of the Columbian Exchange and identify key items exchanged between the Old World and the New World.

Activities:

- **Engage:** Show images or a basket of bananas, potatoes, tomatoes, corn, and chocolate. Ask students where they think these foods originated.
- **Explore:** Discuss the origins and spread of these foods, revealing their historical context.

Assessment:
Exit ticket: List one item from the Columbian Exchange and its origin.

Key Points:

- Introduction to the Columbian Exchange.
- Discussion on the significance of global food systems.

Standard Addressed:
National History Standard: Era 1: The New World and the Age of Exploration.

Day 2: Research and Data Mapping

Objective:
Students will work in teams to research the origin and spread of key crops, animals, diseases, and technologies post-1492.

Activities:

- **Explore:** Students will use a provided dataset to research and plot the movement of items on a world map.
- **Discuss:** Share findings in teams and identify patterns.

Assessment:
Map critique based on accuracy and reasoning.

Key Points:

- Collaborative research on the impact of the Columbian Exchange.
- Visual representation of data.

Standard Addressed:
Geography Standard: Understanding the characteristics and spatial patterns of human populations.

Day 3: Analyzing Impact

Objective:
Students will analyze the long-term effects of the Columbian Exchange on populations, diets, and ecosystems.

Activities:

- **Explain:** Mini-lecture on the significance of the Columbian Exchange, focusing on patterns of population change and ecological impact.
- **Extended Activity:** Students choose an item to research further, creating a cause-effect chain or infographic.

Assessment:
Presentation rubric for the infographic or cause-effect chain.

Key Points:

- Recognition of unintended consequences, such as invasive species and pandemics.
- The interconnectedness of historical events and modern issues.

Standard Addressed:
National History Standard: Era 2: The Age of Revolution.

Day 4: Presentations and Reflection

Objective:
Students will present their research findings and reflect on the significance of the Columbian Exchange.

Activities:

- **Present:** Students showcase their infographics or cause-effect chains to the class.
- **Evaluate:** Conduct a class discussion on long-term effects of the Columbian Exchange.

Assessment:
Peer evaluations of presentations based on clarity and reasoning.

Key Points:

- Encouragement of critical thinking and communication skills.
- Reflection on the ongoing impact of historical events.

Standard Addressed:
STEM Standard: Developing and using models to understand the world.

Culminating Activities Suggestions

1. **Create a Class Gallery:** Display all infographics and maps in a gallery walk where students can view and discuss each other's work.
2. **Debate:** Host a debate on the positive and negative impacts of the Columbian Exchange on modern society.

3. **Write a Reflective Essay:** Students write an essay on how the Columbian Exchange has shaped today's global food systems.

Standards Addressed:

- National History Standards: Era 1 and Era 2.
- Geography Standards: Spatial patterns of populations.
- STEM Standards: Developing models and analyzing data.

This unit plan encompasses the exploration of the Columbian Exchange while integrating STEM concepts and encouraging critical thinking, making it suitable for 8th-grade students.

Assessment Rubric:

Mapping the Spread – The Columbian Exchange

Grades 6–12 Rubric with Point Values (Total: 24 points)

Criteria	4 pts (Excellent)	3 pts (Proficient)	2 pts (Developing)	1 pt (Needs Improvement)
Historical Accuracy	Completely accurate and well-researched	Mostly accurate with minor errors	Some inaccuracies or missing info	Significant factual errors
Geographic Representation	Clear, accurate map showing movement across regions	Mostly accurate map; clear but with minor issues	Some unclear or inaccurate locations	Incomplete or inaccurate geography
Data Use & Interpretation	Thoughtful use of data to show impacts/trends	Uses data clearly but with limited depth	Basic data used; connections unclear	Little or no data used
Visual Clarity & Organization	Organized, easy to follow, enhances message	Mostly clear; some layout issues	Some clutter or confusion	Disorganized or difficult to follow
Explanation of Impact	Strong explanation of multiple effects	Covers key effects with some depth	General or surface-level impacts	Unclear or incomplete explanation
STEM Integration	Demonstrates strong STEM reasoning and systems thinking	STEM connections present but limited	Few STEM ideas; weak systems thinking	No clear STEM integration

Scoring Guide:

22–24: Excellent

18–21: Proficient

14–17: Developing

Below 14: Needs Improvement

Teacher Comments:

Student Reflection: What did you learn about the Columbian Exchange and how STEM helps us understand history?

Simplified Rubric (Grades 3–5 or Quick Check)

Total Possible: 12 points

Category	3 pts – Great Job	2 pts – Getting There	1 pt – Needs Work
Facts	Information is accurate and clear	A few small errors or missing parts	Many mistakes or confusing
Map or Project Design	Looks great and easy to understand	Mostly clear, but a little messy	Hard to read or follow
Use of Data	Shows numbers or facts that support the topic	Some data shown, but not clearly explained	No data or unclear use
Explains Why It Matters	Explains how the Exchange changed the world	Talks about effects, but not in detail	Doesn't explain the impact clearly

Scoring Guide:

- 11–12: Great Job!
- 8–10: Keep Going!
- 4–7: Let's Improve It!

Student Handouts:

Mapping the Spread – The Columbian Exchange

Introduction:

In this activity, you will investigate the Columbian Exchange—the movement of crops, animals, people, and diseases between the Old World and the New World after 1492.

Your Task:

1. Use the data table below to research key items exchanged between continents.
2. Plot their movement on a map using arrows, icons, or color-coding.
3. Choose one item to study further. Create an infographic or short report explaining its journey and impact.
4. Be sure to use data to support your claims—how did this exchange affect population, health, agriculture, or culture?

Data Table: Sample Items in the Columbian Exchange

Item	Origin (Before 1492)	Destination (After 1492)	Impact or Consequences
Potatoes	South America	Europe, Asia, Africa	Improved nutrition, population growth
Horses	Europe	North and South America	Transformed Native cultures and transportation
Smallpox	Europe	Americas	Devastating population decline among Indigenous peoples
Tomatoes	Americas	Europe	Major addition to European cuisine (e.g., Italy)
Sugar Cane	Asia (via Europe)	Caribbean, South America	Drove plantation economies, slave trade
Maize (Corn)	Americas	Europe, Africa, Asia	Staple crop with high yield, supported population growth
Coffee	Africa	Europe and Latin America	Became major trade crop and cultural staple

Reflection Questions:

1. What surprised you most about where common foods and animals came from?

2. How did one item you studied change the environment, economy, or population of the region it spread to?

3. Do you think the Columbian Exchange had more positive or negative effects? Explain your reasoning.

4. How can data and mapping help us understand history better?

Art of STEM

Lesson 2: Revolution by the Numbers – The American Revolution

Why Do We Study Wars?

The Lesson of Revolutions

War is not fun. It's loud, scary, and often heartbreaking. People lose their homes, their families, and sometimes their lives. So you might wonder—why do we spend so much time in school learning about something so sad?

One of the biggest reasons is this: **so we don't make the same mistakes again.**

Take the American Revolution, for example. It happened over 200 years ago, but the decisions made during that time still shape the way we live today. It was a war between the 13 American colonies and the British Empire. But it wasn't just about fighting—it was about ideas: **freedom, fairness, and who gets to help make the rules.**

The colonists were upset. They felt they were being treated unfairly. They had to pay taxes but didn't get a say in how those laws were made. Eventually, their frustration grew into anger, and that anger turned into a revolution—a full-scale war for independence.

But here's the important part: the American Revolution wasn't the first revolution in history, and it wasn't the last.

All over the world, people have stood up to say, "Things need to change." Sometimes change came peacefully. Other times, it came through fighting. Some revolutions made the world better. Others didn't. Every single one has something to teach us.

That's why we study them. Not to celebrate war—but to understand it. To ask **why** it happened. To learn **how** it started. And to figure out **what we can do to avoid another one.**

When we understand the causes of conflict—like unfair laws, inequality, or a lack of communication—we get better at solving problems before they turn into battles. That's how we become wiser leaders and kinder people.

So when you read about the American Revolution, remember: it's more than just history. It's a lesson in standing up for what's right—and working for peace in a world that still needs it.

◯ Discussion Questions

1. Why do you think people study wars, even though they are sad or frightening?
2. What were some of the reasons the American colonists wanted independence from Britain?
3. Do you think a revolution always has to be violent? Why or why not?
4. What are some ways people can solve problems peacefully before they turn into conflict?
5. Can you think of a time in your own life or community when someone stood up for fairness or change?
6. Why is it important to learn from the mistakes of the past?
7. If you could talk to someone who lived during the American Revolution, what would you want to ask them?

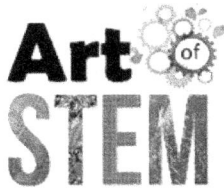

Lesson 2: Revolution by the Numbers – The American Revolution

Topic: Economic and logistical factors in the American Revolution

STEM Focus: Data interpretation, modeling supply chains, budgeting, logistics

Subjects: U.S. History, Economics, Civics, Math

✉ Teacher Letter

Dear Educator,

This lesson takes a fresh approach to teaching the American Revolution—not only as a political and ideological movement but as a complex logistical and economic undertaking. By analyzing troop movement, supply costs, and resource allocation, students apply data-driven reasoning and systems thinking to deepen their understanding of this critical period.

Integrating STEM into your history classroom is not about turning students into engineers—it's about helping them think like analysts, planners, and decision-makers. This lesson demonstrates to students how the war was won not just on battlefields, but also through effective planning, budgeting, and resource management.

This template demonstrates how data collection and project-based learning can enhance traditional instruction. It invites students to engage with history as a living system shaped by tangible constraints and real-world decisions—just like today.

Warm regards,

Beverly Simmons
Author, Educator, Curriculum Developer
STEMConnector's 100 Women Leaders in STEM
State Department International STEM Speaker

5E Lesson Plan: Revolution by the Numbers

Engage

Scenario Prompt:
Present this question: *"What does it take to fight a war—besides soldiers?"*
Show students a historical supply list: tents, powder, uniforms, food, horses.

Class Discussion:

- What would it take to equip and feed a group of 100 soldiers?
- What might go wrong if supplies are delayed?

Explore

This lesson integrates STEM skills with historical content to help students view the American Revolution as a complex system shaped by economics, geography, and logistics, rather than just battles and politics. It encourages analytical thinking and real-world problem solving across disciplines.

Activity:
Students receive a simplified dataset of supplies needed by the Continental Army and their costs in pounds/dollars. Example items: uniforms, muskets, rations, horseshoes.

Task:
Working in teams, students must "supply" an army of 200 soldiers for a month within a set budget. They calculate quantities, costs, and discuss trade-offs.

Optional STEM Extension:
Plot troop movements and supply routes on a map. How might distance and geography affect supply lines?

Explain

Teacher-Guided Discussion:
Explain the economic limitations of the Continental Congress. Discuss the importance of local militia contributions and supply shortages.

Mini-Lecture:
Explore key logistical challenges during the Revolution:

- No centralized army funding
- British naval blockades
- Harsh winter conditions (Valley Forge)

Extend

Project Options:

- Create a historical infographic comparing British and Colonial military spending and resource access
- Design a "Continental Army Logistics Plan" including maps, supply needs, and risk assessment
- Use spreadsheets to simulate and visualize the cost of sustaining the war

STEM Focus:
Systems thinking, budgeting, mathematical reasoning, geographic awareness

Evaluate

Assessment Options:

- Group presentations of their logistics plan
- Math-based reflection: How did budgeting affect decision-making?
- Written response: How did economic and logistical factors influence the war's outcome?

4-Day Unit Plan: Revolution by the Numbers

Unit Duration: 4 School Days
Grade Level: Adaptable for Middle-High
Topic: Economic and logistical factors in the American Revolution
STEM Focus: Data interpretation, Modeling supply chains, Budgeting, Logistics, Systems thinking, Mathematical reasoning, Geographic awareness
Subject Areas: U.S. History, Economics, Civics, Math

Day 1: Engage and Explore

Objective:
Students will understand the various supplies required for an army and discuss the implications of supply shortages during the Revolutionary War.

Activities:

- **Scenario Prompt:** Present the question, "What does it take to fight a war—besides soldiers?"
- **Supply List Discussion:** Show a historical supply list (tents, powder, uniforms, food, horses).
- Class Discussion:
    - What would it take to equip and feed a group of 100 soldiers?
    - What might go wrong if supplies are delayed?

Suggested Assessment:
Participation in class discussions.

Key Points:

- Importance of logistics in warfare.
- Initial understanding of supply needs.

Standard Addressed:
CCSS.ELA-LITERACY.SL.6.1: Engage effectively in a range of collaborative discussions.

Day 2: Explore and Explain

Objective:
Students will work in teams to calculate and plan supplies for an army of 200 soldiers within a budget.

Activities:

- Group Activity:
    - Distribute simplified datasets of supplies needed by the Continental Army and their costs.
    - Teams will calculate quantities and costs to supply 200 soldiers for a month within the budget.
- Optional STEM Extension:
    - Plot troop movements and supply routes on a map. Discuss how distance and geography affect supply lines.

Suggested Assessment:
Completion of the supply plan with calculations.

Key Points:

- Teamwork and collaboration in problem-solving.
- Basic budgeting and calculations.

Standard Addressed:
CCSS.MATH.CONTENT.6.RP.A.3: Use ratio and rate reasoning to solve real-world and mathematical problems.

Day 3: Explain and Extend

Objective:
Students will explore the economic limitations faced by the Continental Congress and logistical challenges during the Revolutionary War.

Activities:

- Teacher-Guided Discussion:
    - Discuss economic limitations and local militia contributions.
    - Review logistical challenges (no centralized funding, British blockades, winter conditions).
- Mini-Lecture:

        ○   Present key logistical challenges faced during the Revolution.

Suggested Assessment:
Reflection on key logistical challenges discussed in class.

Key Points:

- Understanding the economic factors affecting the war.
- Importance of local contributions.

Standard Addressed:
SS.H.6.3.1: Analyze the causes and effects of historical events.

Day 4: Evaluate and Present

Objective:
Students will present their logistics plans and reflect on the impact of budgeting on decision-making.

Activities:

- Group Presentations:
    - Each team presents its logistics plan, discussing the supplies needed and its budget.
- Math-Based Reflection:
    - Discuss how budgeting affected their decision-making.
- Written Response:
    - Reflect on how economic and logistical factors influenced the war's outcome.

Suggested Assessment:
Group presentations and written reflections.

Key Points:

- Application of mathematical reasoning in a historical context.
- Reflection on the influence of logistics on historical events.

Standard Addressed:
CCSS.ELA-LITERACY.W.6.1: Write arguments to support claims in an analysis of substantive topics or texts.

Culminating Activities Suggestions

1. **Create a Historical Infographic:** Compare British and Colonial military spending and resource access.
2. **Design a Logistics Plan:** Include maps, supply needs, and risk assessments for the Continental Army.
3. **Spreadsheet Simulation:** Use spreadsheets to simulate and visualize the cost of sustaining the war.

Standards Addressed:

NCSS D2.His.3.6-8: Analyze the relationships among multiple historical developments.
CCSS.MATH.CONTENT.7.RP.A.1: Analyze proportional relationships and use them to solve real-world problems.
NCSS D2.His.12.6-8: Evaluate the significance of historical events.
CCSS.ELA-LITERACY.WHST.6-8.7: Conduct short research projects to answer a question.

Across the Curriculum Ideas:

1. History / Social Studies:

Analyze the political and economic challenges faced by the Continental Congress.
Discuss the role of local militias and community contributions in sustaining the war effort.
Explore the impact of British naval blockades and harsh weather on the Revolutionary War.
Study troop movements and geography's influence on logistics and strategy.

2. Mathematics:

Calculate quantities and costs of supplies needed for troops.
Work within budgeting constraints to plan supply purchases.
Use spreadsheets to simulate costs and visualize data.
Interpret datasets of supply needs and expenses.
Analyze trade-offs between different types of supplies and their costs.

3. Economics:

Understand budgeting and resource allocation in wartime.
Compare military spending of the British vs. Colonial forces.
Explore economic limitations and their impact on war outcomes.
Analyze supply chain challenges and their effects on military readiness.

4. Civics:

Discuss the role of governance and Congress in managing resources.
Explore decision-making processes in crisis situations.
Reflect on how economic pressures influenced political actions during the Revolution.

5. Geography / STEM Extension:

Map troop movements and supply routes.
Analyze how geography and distance affected supply lines and logistics.
Discuss environmental factors like winter conditions in Valley Forge.

General Suggested Activities Integrating STEM and History Studies of Revolutions and Conflicts Throughout History:

Data-Driven Supply Planning: Students calculate supply needs, costs, and trade-offs for a Continental Army unit, reinforcing budgeting and arithmetic skills.

Mapping Logistics: Plot supply routes and troop movements on maps, linking geography with military strategy and logistics.

Infographic Project: Create visual comparisons of British and Colonial military spending, integrating data interpretation and historical analysis.

Simulation with Spreadsheets: Model the cost of sustaining the war and experiment with scenarios, fostering systems thinking and economic reasoning.

Group Presentations: Share logistics plans demonstrating understanding of history, math, and economics.

Rubric: Revolution by the Numbers – The American Revolution

Grades 6–12 Rubric with Point Values (Total: 24 points)

Criteria	4 pts (Excellent)	3 pts (Proficient)	2 pts (Developing)	1 pt (Needs Improvement)
Historical Understanding	Shows deep understanding of logistical/economic factors in the war	Understands key ideas with minor gaps	Basic understanding; some confusion	Little understanding of historical context
Budgeting & Calculations	Accurate math and clear cost trade-offs	Minor errors; mostly sound budgeting	Inconsistent or unclear math	Major errors or missing calculations
Decision-Making & Justification	Well-justified choices supported by data	Some reasoning shown; mostly logical	Reasoning unclear or weakly supported	Little or no justification provided
Visual Organization	Clear, engaging layout (infographic/map/table)	Mostly clear with minor layout issues	Cluttered or somewhat confusing	Hard to follow or incomplete visual
Connection to Real-World Challenges	Strong connection to real-world logistics or planning	Some clear connections made	Few or vague real-world links	No evident connection to modern or practical planning
STEM Integration	Excellent use of STEM skills (math, modeling, mapping)	Good use with minor gaps	Limited STEM application	Little or no STEM elements included

Scoring Guide:

22–24: Excellent

18–21: Proficient

14–17: Developing

Below 14: Needs Improvement

Teacher Comments:

Student Reflection: What did you learn about how data and planning helped win the American Revolution?

Simplified Rubric (Grades 3–5)

Total Possible: 12 points

Category	3 pts – Great Job	2 pts – Getting There	1 pt – Needs Work
Facts & History	Accurate facts and war ideas are clear	Mostly right with small mistakes	Many mistakes or missing info
Math & Supplies	Math is right and fits budget	Mostly correct but a bit off	Math is wrong or missing
Planning Choices	Explains supply choices well	Some explanation, not all clear	Hard to understand or no reason given
Neatness & Design	Easy to read and understand	Mostly clear with small issues	Messy or hard to read

Scoring Guide:

11–12: Great Job!

8–10: Keep Going!

4–7: Let's Improve It!

Student Handouts:
The American "Revolution by the Numbers"

Introduction:

Imagine you're part of the Continental Congress during the American Revolution. You've been asked to supply 200 soldiers for one month. Your challenge: plan what they'll need, stay within budget, and explain your decisions.

Your Task:

1. Review the supply list and costs below.
2. Decide how many of each item your troops will need.
3. Calculate the total cost. Your budget is $10,000.
4. Create a simple chart, infographic, or map to explain your supply choices.
5. Reflect: How did planning and budgeting affect your decisions?

Continental Army Supply List

Item	Unit Cost	Suggested Qty per Soldier	Your Quantity
Ration Pack (1 week)	$15	4	
Uniform (Shirt, Pants, Coat)	$50	1	
Musket & Ammo Pack	$150	1	
Blanket	$12	1	
Shoes	$20	1	
Tent (1 per 4 soldiers)	$100	0.25	
Horse (for officers)	$300	0.05	
Medical Supplies (per soldier)	$30	1	

Reflection Questions:

1. What was the most difficult part of staying within your budget?

2. Which items did you choose to prioritize? Why

3. How do you think supply problems affected the Continental Army in real life?

4. How did using math and data help you understand this part of history?

Art of STEM

Lesson 3: Factory Data – Industrialization and Urban Growth

🏭 "Smoke and Sparks"

A Letter from the City of Change

Dear Future Reader,

If you're holding this letter, then you've found the message I hid in the bricks of Milltown's first chimney.

Let me introduce myself. My name is Elsie Watts. I'm twelve years old and I live in a city that never sleeps. Or at least, the machines don't. The gears turn day and night, the hammers pound, and the smokestacks puff like giant black candles.

Just ten years ago, Milltown was a quiet village with more sheep than people. Now? It's all factories, trains, and people—*so many people.*

My father works at the textile mill, pulling long shifts with hundreds of others. My mother mends shirts for shopkeepers and tries to keep the coal dust off the laundry. I help deliver hot tea to the workers in the morning and read at night by lanternlight—when there's time.

Some people say the machines are magic. That they've turned us from farmers to inventors. And it's true—the machines make cloth faster, build houses taller, and send letters like this one further than we ever dreamed.

But not everything feels magical. The air smells like smoke. The river runs slower, darker. I used to catch frogs there. Now I just see oil-slicked ripples. Some kids my age work full shifts in the factory. Others cough a lot.

It's strange, living in a time when *everything* is changing. One week there's a new bridge. The next, a new train. It's exciting—but also confusing. Are we building something better… or just something bigger?

That's why I'm writing this letter to you. Maybe in your time, you can look back and see the full picture. Maybe your schools teach about us—not just the machines, but the people. The choices. The consequences.

If you study our story, maybe your cities will grow smarter. Maybe you'll find ways to invent without polluting. To power up without burning out.

So study the factories. The smoke. The numbers. But also—study the people. Learn from us, not just about us.

Yours in coal dust and curiosity,

Elsie Watts

Milltown, 1845

Discussion Questions: The Industrial Revolution

1. **What stood out to you in Elsie's letter?**
   o What words or images helped you imagine her life in Milltown?
2. **How did life change for Elsie and her family during the Industrial Revolution?**
   o What were the good and bad parts of those changes?
3. **Why do you think Elsie described the machines as both "magic" and "confusing"?**
   o Can something be helpful and harmful at the same time?
4. **What were some of the environmental changes Elsie noticed?**
   o What did the river used to be like? What changed?
5. **How do you think data (like factory output or population growth) could help tell the full story of the Industrial Revolution?**
   o What kinds of patterns might we look for in data?
6. **If you were living in Milltown in 1845, what job might you have had?**
   o Would you be excited or nervous about the changes happening around you?
7. **Why does Elsie want people in the future to study the Industrial Revolution?**
   o What does she hope we learn from it?

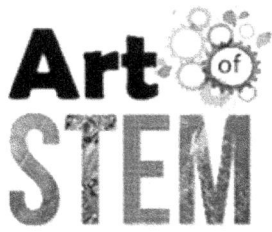

Lesson 3: Factory Data – Industrialization and Urban Growth

Factory Data – Industrialization and Urban Growth
Topic: The Industrial Revolution and its impact on cities and workers
STEM Focus: Data interpretation, population mapping, economic modeling, environmental science
Subjects: U.S. History, World History, Geography, Economics, Civics

💜 Teacher Letter

Dear Educator,

This lesson connects the sweeping historical changes of the Industrial Revolution with the measurable, visual impact it had on cities, workers, and the environment. Using historical data, students track population growth, factory output, and living conditions to better understand how industrialization transformed societies—and created the blueprint for modern urban life.

This is an ideal example of how STEM supports social studies instruction. By interpreting graphs, maps, and labor statistics, students gain analytical tools that bring historical patterns to life. They don't just read about crowding and pollution—they see it, measure it, and model it.

Project-based learning allows students to propose city redesigns or workplace reforms that are historically informed and data-driven, building both empathy and problem-solving skills.

Let's teach students not just what happened in the past—but how to analyze it like historians, scientists, and civic leaders.

Warmly,

Beverly Simmons | Author, Educator, Curriculum Developer

5E Lesson Plan: Factory Data – Industrialization and Urban Growth

Engage

Visual Prompt:

Show side-by-side images of a rural village and an industrial city c. 1850. Ask:
What do you notice about each environment?
How might daily life be different in each?

Explore

Activity:

Students receive historical data tables (simplified) on:
Urban population growth (e.g., Manchester, New York, Chicago)
Factory output over time
Working hours and wages
Pollution/coal consumption

Task:

Students graph at least one set of data and analyze patterns over time. What trends do they observe?

Explain

Mini-Lecture or Guided Discussion:

Discuss connections between factory output, urbanization, and working conditions.
Introduce the concept of externalities—unintended environmental and health impacts.

Key ideas:

Industrialization fueled urban growth

Economic gains came with human and environmental costs
Early cities were rarely planned—leading to overcrowding and poor sanitation

Extend

Project Options:

Redesign an 1850s industrial city for better public health and sustainability
Create an infographic comparing worker life before and after industrialization
Analyze coal consumption and propose early alternative energy strategies

STEM Focus:

Mapping, graphing, system modeling, social reform design based on data

Evaluate

Assessment Options:
Presentation of city redesign or reform proposal
Written reflection: How did data help you understand industrialization differently?
Peer review of infographics based on clarity, accuracy, and insightTopic: Expansion of voting rights in the U.S. and its impact on participation

STEM Focus: Data analysis, visualization, demographics, timeline modeling

Subjects: U.S. History, Civics, Political Science, Math

Factory Data Unit Plan

Unit Duration: 5 School Days
Grade Level: 8th Grade
Subjects: U.S. History, World History, Geography, Economics, Civics
STEM Focus: Data interpretation, population mapping, economic modeling, environmental science

---

Day 1: Introduction to Industrialization and Urban Growth

Objective:
Students will understand the key concepts of industrialization and its impact on urban growth through visual prompts.

Activities:

- **Engage:** Show side-by-side images of a rural village and an industrial city c. 1850.
  - Discussion Questions:
  - What do you notice about each environment?
  - How might daily life be different in each?

Assessment:
Class participation in discussion.

Key Points:

- Initial understanding of industrialization and urban environments.
- Importance of visual aids in historical analysis.

Standard Addressed:
National History Standard 8.3: Analyze the effects of industrialization on urban life.

Day 2: Exploring Historical Data

Objective:
Students will analyze historical data related to urban population growth, factory output, working conditions, and pollution.

Activities:

Explore:

- Distribute simplified historical data tables on:
- Urban population growth (Manchester, New York, Chicago)
- Factory output over time
- Working hours and wages
- Pollution/coal consumption
- Task: Graph at least one set of data and analyze observed trends.

Assessment:
Completion of graphs and observations.

Key Points:

- Understanding data representation.
- Identifying trends and patterns in historical context.

Standard Addressed:
National Geography Standard 7: Understand how human actions modify the physical environment.

Day 3: Connections and Impact

Objective:
Students will articulate the connections between factory output, urbanization, and working conditions.

Activities:

Explain:

- Mini-lecture on connections between industrialization, urban growth, and externalities.
- Key Ideas:
- Industrialization fueled urban growth.
- Economic gains came with human and environmental costs.
- Early cities faced overcrowding and poor sanitation.

Assessment:
Written notes and participation in discussion.

Key Points:

- The dual nature of industrialization's impact—economic vs. environmental.
- Introduction of externalities as an essential concept.

Standard Addressed:
Civics Standard 6.2: Analyze how social, political, and economic factors influence the development of policies.

Day 4: Project Work

Objective:
Students will apply their knowledge to a project that redesigns an industrial city or compares worker life pre- and post-industrialization.

Activities:

Extend:

- Project Options:
- Redesign an 1850s industrial city for better public health and sustainability.
- Create an infographic comparing worker life before and after industrialization.
- Analyze coal consumption and propose early alternative energy strategies.

Assessment:
Draft of project proposals and peer feedback.

Key Points:

- Application of historical knowledge to modern contexts.
- Emphasizing creativity and problem-solving in design.

Standard Addressed:
National Economics Standard 8: Understand the role of incentives in economic decision-making.

Day 5: Presentations and Reflections

Objective:
Students will present their projects and reflect on their learning regarding industrialization.

Activities:

Evaluate:

- Present proposals or projects to the class.
- Written reflection: How did data help you understand industrialization differently?
- Peer review of infographics based on clarity, accuracy, and insight.

Assessment:
Presentation performance and written reflection.

Key Points:

- Reinforcement of learning through presentation.
- Emphasis on peer feedback and self-reflection.

Standard Addressed:
National History Standard 8.6: Analyze the significance of historical events and themes.

Culminating Activities Suggestions

1. **City Redesign Competition:** Students will present their redesigned industrial city and explain how their modifications improve public health and sustainability.
2. **Infographic Gallery Walk:** Create a gallery of infographics comparing worker life before and after industrialization for students to review and discuss.
3. **Debate on Energy Strategies:** Hold a classroom debate on the effectiveness of proposed alternative energy strategies versus coal consumption.

Standards Addressed:

- National History Standards
- National Geography Standards
- National Economics Standards
- Civics Standards
- STEM Standards: Engineering Design, Data Analysis, and Environmental Science Principles.

Rubric: Factory Data – Industrialization and Urban Growth

Grades 6–12 Rubric with Point Values (Total: 24 points)

Criteria	4 pts (Excellent)	3 pts (Proficient)	2 pts (Developing)	1 pt (Needs Improvement)
Data Accuracy & Interpretation	Data is correctly used and trends are clearly explained	Data mostly accurate; trends are discussed	Some data is used; explanation unclear	Inaccurate or missing data use
Historical Understanding	Deep understanding of industrial impacts shown	Good understanding with some minor gaps	Basic grasp of topic with oversights	Little evidence of historical understanding
Visual Representation (Graph/Map/Infographic)	Well-organized and clear; enhances understanding	Mostly clear with minor layout issues	Somewhat confusing or disorganized	Disorganized or lacks clarity
Problem-Solving or Reform Plan	Creative and data-driven redesign or reform idea	Plausible idea with some connection to data	Limited proposal; weak data connection	Missing or unrealistic proposal
Connection to STEM Concepts	Strong integration of STEM skills (graphing, modeling)	STEM used with minor gaps	Basic or unclear STEM connection	STEM not meaningfully applied
Clarity & Communication	Project is clearly communicated and engaging	Mostly clear with a few weak spots	Hard to follow in places	Unclear or poorly presented

Scoring Guide:

22–24: Excellent

18–21: Proficient
14–17: Developing
Below 14: Needs Improvement

Teacher Comments:

Student Reflection: What did you learn about how industrialization changed cities and lives—and how data helps reveal those changes?

Simplified Rubric (Grades 3–5)

Total Possible: 12 points

Category	3 pts – Great Job	2 pts – Getting There	1 pt – Needs Work
Graphs or Charts	Graph is neat and shows changes over time	Some data shown, a little confusing	Missing or incorrect graph
Facts About Factories	Shows clear ideas about how life changed	Some good points, a few errors	Hard to understand or off-topic
City Plan or Idea	Good solution that fits the time period	Interesting but not clear	Unrealistic or not explained
Neatness & Explanation	Easy to read and follow	Mostly clear	Hard to follow or sloppy

Scoring Guide:

11–12: Great Job!

8–10: Keep Going!

4–7: Let's Improve It!

Student Handouts: Factory Data – Industrialization and Urban Growth

Introduction:

During the Industrial Revolution, cities grew rapidly as factories began to change the way people lived and worked. In this activity, you'll use historical data to explore the effects of industrialization on urban growth, the environment, and worker conditions.

Your Task:

1. Review the data sets below (population, factory output, coal use, wages).

2. Choose one or more to graph and interpret. What trends do you see?

3. Based on what you learn, design a solution: redesign a city, propose a reform, or create an infographic about life during industrialization.

4. Reflect on how industrialization affected people, cities, and the environment.

Data Set 1: Urban Population Growth (Sample Cities)

City	1800	1850	1900
Manchester (UK)	90,000	300,000	645,000
New York City (USA)	60,000	515,000	3,437,000
Chicago (USA)	None	30,000	1,698,000

Data Set 2: Average Working Hours per Week

Year	Factory Workers	Child Laborers
1820	72	70
1850	68	60
1880	60	48

Data Set 3: Coal Use and Air Pollution

Year	Coal Consumed (tons)	Reported Air Pollution Events

1800	1.2 million	20
1850	5.6 million	70
1900	12.3 million	160

Reflection Questions:

1. What trends did you notice in the population, labor, or pollution data?

2. How did life in cities change during the Industrial Revolution?

3. What challenges would you face if you lived in a factory town in 1850?

4. What solutions or reforms might improve life during this time?

Art of STEM

Lesson 4: Voting Through the Decades – Rights, Access & Turnout

"The First Time We Voted"

A Story to Introduce Voting Rights & Participation

My grandma keeps a little envelope in the back of her photo album. It's old, yellowed, and sealed with a single piece of tape. On the front, in her loopy handwriting, it says:

"The First Time We Voted."

I asked her about it once, and she smiled like it was a memory wrapped in sunshine and struggle. "That envelope," she said, "holds a photo of your great-grandmother and me, right after we cast our first ballots. We were crying—tears of joy."

I didn't understand at first. "Didn't everyone always get to vote?"

That made her laugh—a warm, wise kind of laugh. "Oh honey, no. The right to vote wasn't given to everyone. It was earned. Fought for. Demanded."

She told me about the long lines and literacy tests, about people being turned away or told they weren't "ready." About how laws didn't always mean freedom for everyone. About marches and protests and bravery.

I listened, wide-eyed, trying to imagine a time when voices like mine, like hers, like ours— weren't allowed to count.

"Voting is more than a choice," she said. "It's a voice. It's power. It's hope."

Now every time we go to vote, my grandma wears the same pin she wore that day in the photo. It says **"Let Us Vote."**

I hold her hand as we walk into the polling station, and I picture all the footsteps that came before ours. People of every color, every gender, every background—fighting to be heard.

This year in school, we're learning how voting rights have changed over time. We're looking at timelines and data—when certain groups gained access, and how many people showed up. Some years, the numbers go up. Some years, they fall.

But the story behind those numbers? That's the part I understand best.

Because in my family, voting isn't just a civic duty. It's a family tradition. A celebration of voices that weren't always welcome.

And someday, when I'm old enough, I'll add a photo to that envelope in the back of the album. It'll say:

"The First Time *I* Voted."

📋 Voting Rights in U.S. History: A Timeline

1776 – *Only white, male landowners can vote*

- Early voting laws were based on property ownership, race, and gender.

1870 – *15th Amendment: African American men gain the right to vote*

- "The right to vote shall not be denied… on account of race, color, or previous condition of servitude."

1920 – *19th Amendment: Women gain the right to vote*

- After decades of activism, women win the legal right to vote in national elections.

1924 – *Indian Citizenship Act grants Native Americans U.S. citizenship and voting rights*

- But many states still found ways to block Native voting until the 1960s.

1965 – *Voting Rights Act bans racial discrimination in voting*

- This landmark law ended unfair practices like literacy tests and poll taxes.

1971 – *26th Amendment: Voting age lowered from 21 to 18*

- Sparked by young Americans fighting in the Vietnam War but unable to vote.

2013 – *Supreme Court ruling weakens the Voting Rights Act*

- Some states begin passing laws like voter ID requirements, which make it harder for some groups to vote.

Today – *Voting rights are still debated and changing*

- Some people work to expand access; others call for more restrictions. Participation and policy go hand in hand.

Activity Ideas:

- **Classroom Timeline Wall:** Have students create visual "milestone cards" for each date with illustrations or photos.
- **Data Dive:** Have students look up voter turnout data for different years and discuss trends.
- **"Then & Now" Compare/Contrast:** How has who *can* vote changed? What still needs to change?

Art of STEM

Lesson 4: Voting Through the Decades – Rights, Access & Turnout

Topic: Expansion of voting rights in the U.S. and its impact on participation
STEM Focus: Data analysis, visualization, demographics, timeline modeling
Subjects: U.S. History, Civics, Political Science, Math

💌 Teacher Letter

Dear Educator,

This lesson invites students to explore the powerful connection between policy and participation by examining how voting rights have expanded—and been restricted—throughout U.S. history. Students engage with real historical data on voter turnout and demographics, making this a hands-on opportunity to apply statistical thinking and timeline modeling to one of the most vital aspects of civic life.

Incorporating STEM in social studies doesn't just strengthen skills—it makes learning more equitable. By analyzing who could vote vs. who did, students uncover patterns that reflect systemic change and raise critical questions about fairness, access, and democracy.

Whether they're interpreting graphs or building infographics, your students will walk away with both civic knowledge and real-world data literacy—exactly what we want for the next generation of voters and leaders.Warmly,

Beverly Simmons

Author, Educator, Curriculum Developer

5E Lesson Plan:
Voting Through the Decades

Engage

Prompt:

Ask students: "Should voter turnout be used to measure the health of a democracy?" Show graphs of voter turnout during U.S. presidential elections from different decades.

Quick Reflection:
What patterns do you notice?
What might explain the dips and spikes?

Explore

Activity:

Students receive a simplified data set on:
> Voting eligibility by group (gender, race, age, etc.) over time
> Turnout rates in selected presidential elections
> Laws or amendments that expanded (or restricted) access

Task:

Students graph changes in turnout or eligibility over time. Annotate their graphs with historical milestones (e.g., 15th, 19th, 24th Amendments, VRA of 1965).

Explain

Teacher-Guided Discussion:
Discuss:

> How have voting rights changed over time?

What's the difference between the right to vote and the ability to vote (e.g., registration, voter ID laws)?

How do turnout and access reflect broader social trends?

Extend

Project Options:

Create a timeline infographic of voter access milestones

Design a PSA using turnout data to encourage civic participation

Map out a strategy to improve youth voter turnout using recent statistics

STEM Focus:

Visual data presentation, graphing, policy modeling, using census data or turnout datasets

Evaluate

Assessment Options:

Group timeline or infographic presentation

Short essay or reflection on what influences voting behavior

Peer review of graphs and how well they explain change over time

STEM Focus: Data analysis, visualization, demographics, timeline modeling

Subjects: U.S. History, Civics, Political Science, Math

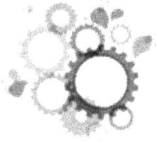

Voting Through The Decades Unit Plan

Day 1: Engage and Explore

Objective: Students will analyze voter turnout data from various decades to identify patterns and trends in U.S. democracy.

Activities:

- Introduce the question: "Should voter turnout be used to measure the health of a democracy?"
- Present graphs of voter turnout during U.S. presidential elections.
- Facilitate a quick reflection on observed patterns.
- Distribute simplified data sets on voting eligibility and turnout rates.
- Students will graph changes in turnout or eligibility over time, annotating their graphs with historical milestones (e.g., 15th, 19th Amendments).

Assessment: Graphs will be reviewed for accuracy and clarity.
Key Points: Understanding the significance of voter turnout as a measure of democracy.
Standard Addressed: C3 Framework for Social Studies State Standards - D2.Civ.11.6-8.

Day 2: Explain and Discuss

Objective: Students will understand the historical context of voting rights and the difference between the right to vote and the ability to vote.

Activities:

- Engage students in a teacher-guided discussion on how voting rights have changed over time.
- Discuss the implications of voter ID laws and registration barriers.
- Analyze how turnout rates reflect broader social trends.
- Assessment: Participation in class discussion and submission of reflection notes.
- Key Points: Differentiating between the right to vote and the ability to vote.

Standard Addressed: National Council for the Social Studies - Theme 10: Civic Ideals and Practices.

Day 3: Extend - Project Options

Objective: Students will apply their understanding of voting rights by creating informative and persuasive presentations.

Activities:

- Introduce project options:
    1. Create a timeline infographic of voter access milestones.
    2. Design a PSA using turnout data to encourage civic participation.
    3. Map out a strategy to improve youth voter turnout using statistics.
- Students will work in groups to develop their projects.
  Assessment: Group project presentation and peer feedback.
  Key Points: Importance of civic engagement and strategies to improve participation.
  Standard Addressed: Common Core State Standards - ELA Literacy: Speaking and Listening - SL.8.1.

Day 4: Evaluate and Reflect

Objective: Students will evaluate their understanding of voting rights and their impact on civic engagement.

Activities:

- Present group projects to the class.
- Conduct a peer review of graphs and project presentations.
- Assign a short essay reflecting on factors influencing voting behavior.
  Assessment: Completion of essays and peer review feedback forms.
  Key Points: Analyzing the impact of historical and contemporary factors on voter turnout.
  Standard Addressed: Mathematics Standards - Statistics and Probability - 8.SP.A.1.

Culminating Activities Suggestions

1. Host a debate on the importance of voting rights and their impact on society.
2. Create a class mural that visually represents the history of voting rights in the U.S.
3. Organize a mock election to practice civic engagement and understand the voting process.

Standards Addressed:

- C3 Framework for Social Studies State Standards
- National Council for the Social Studies - Theme 10: Civic Ideals and Practices
- Common Core State Standards - ELA Literacy: Speaking and Listening
- Mathematics Standards - Statistics and Probability

Rubric: Voting Through the Decades – Rights, Access & Turnout

Grades 6–12 Rubric with Point Values (Total: 24 points)

Criteria	4 pts (Excellent)	3 pts (Proficient)	2 pts (Developing)	1 pt (Needs Improvement)
Historical Understanding	Clearly explains changes in voting rights and turnout	Good understanding with minor gaps	Basic understanding; some confusion	Limited or inaccurate understanding
Data Interpretation	Accurate use of data with strong insight	Correct data use; trends mostly explained	Some correct data; explanation unclear	Inaccurate or missing data use
Visual Representation (Graph/Timeline)	Clear, accurate, and engaging visual work	Mostly clear with a few layout issues	Somewhat confusing or missing detail	Unclear or lacks required elements
Civic Connection	Connects voting trends to broader civic change	Makes some good civic connections	Basic or weakly supported connections	No real connection made
STEM Integration	Excellent use of graphing, modeling, or data tools	Good STEM use with minor gaps	Basic STEM use, limited insight	Little or no STEM integration shown
Communication & Clarity	Project is well-structured and easy to understand	Mostly clear; some weak spots	Hard to follow in places	Unclear or poorly communicated

Scoring Guide:

22–24: Excellent

18–21: Proficient

14–17: Developing

Below 14: Needs Improvement

Teacher Comments:

Student Reflection: How has the right to vote changed over time, and what can data teach us about equity and democracy?

Simplified Rubric (Grades 3–5)

Total Possible: 12 points

Category	3 pts – Great Job	2 pts – Getting There	1 pt – Needs Work
Facts About Voting	Shows when and how rights changed	Some good info, small mistakes	Missing or incorrect facts
Graphs or Timeline	Easy to read and matches the facts	Mostly clear, some parts unclear	Hard to read or missing
Civic Message	Clear message about voting or change	Basic idea shared	Message missing or confusing
Neatness & Effort	Well organized and neat	Some effort shown	Messy or rushed work

Scoring Guide:

11–12: Great Job!

8–10: Keep Going!

4–7: Let's Improve It!

Student Handouts: Voting Through the Decades – Rights, Access & Turnout

Introduction:

Voting is a key part of democracy—but not everyone has always had the right to vote. In this lesson, you'll use historical data to track how voting rights and turnout have changed over time in the United States.

Your Task:

1. Review the historical data sets provided below.
2. Choose one to graph or chart and identify key patterns.
3. Annotate your graph or timeline with major changes in voting rights (amendments, laws, movements).
4. Reflect on how voting access affects civic participation.

Data Set 1: Voter Turnout in Presidential Elections (%)

Election Year	Eligible Voters Turnout (%)	Notes
1828	57.6%	White male landowners only
1876	81.8%	Post-Civil War, some Black men vote
1920	49.2%	First election after women gained the vote
1964	61.9%	Before Voting Rights Act
1968	60.8%	After VRA of 1965
1996	49.0%	One of the lowest turnouts
2020	66.8%	High turnout during pandemic

Data Set 2: Major Voting Rights Milestones

Year	Voting Change
1870	15th Amendment: Vote extended to Black men
1920	19th Amendment: Women gain the right to vote
1965	Voting Rights Act bans literacy tests
1971	26th Amendment: Lowers voting age to 18
2013	Supreme Court weakens VRA protections

Reflection Questions:

1. What patterns do you notice in the turnout data?

2. Which voting rights changes made the biggest difference?

3. What might prevent people from voting even if they have the legal right?

4. What ideas do you have for encouraging voter turnout today?

Lesson 5: Mapping Empires – Power, Trade & Technology in Global History

🌐 "The Mapmaker's Apprentice"

A Story to Introduce Empires, Trade, and Global Exchange

Kavi ran his fingers over the old parchment map, eyes wide with wonder. Curled edges, inked coastlines, and faint trade routes stretched like spiderwebs across oceans and continents.

"Where does this one go?" he asked, pointing to a bold red line snaking across Asia.

"Silk Road," his grandfather replied, adjusting his spectacles. "Camel caravans once carried silk, spices, even ideas along that very trail."

Kavi was spending the summer with his grandfather, a retired mapmaker and collector of ancient atlases. His tiny apartment was stacked with rolled scrolls and dusty globes. It smelled like ink, old paper, and adventure.

"You see," Grandfather said, unfurling another map, "empires didn't just conquer land. They controlled the flow of everything—salt, gold, sugar, books, even languages."

Kavi traced another route—this one stretched from West Africa across the Sahara. "What's this line?"

"That's the trans-Saharan trade route. Empires like Mali and Songhai used it to move gold, salt, and knowledge. Timbuktu wasn't just a funny name—it was a center of learning."

Kavi's mind buzzed. He'd always thought of empires as armies and castles. But now, he saw them as invisible systems, like giant machines powered by roads and rivers and ships.

"What about the people?" Kavi asked. "Did they move, too?"

Grandfather's eyes grew serious. "Yes. Sometimes willingly—merchants, pilgrims, explorers. But sometimes not. Many were enslaved, taken by force. Empires moved people as if they were cargo. That's part of the story too."

Kavi stared at the globe, noticing how close the continents were in some places—and how far in others. "So geography decides everything?"

"Geography gives choices," Grandfather said. "But empires decide how to use them."

Kavi leaned back, imagining ships crossing seas, spices tucked into sacks, messages hidden in scrolls. "What would the world look like without those routes?" he asked.

"Very different," Grandfather said. "Empires shaped the paths we walk—even today. You use words, wear clothes, and eat foods from places you've never even been to."

Kavi opened his notebook and started sketching his own map, drawing arrows from continent to continent. "Can I make my own trade network?" he asked.

"Of course," Grandfather said. "But remember—what you connect can change everything."

🌍 Guiding Questions: Empires and Global Exchange

1. **Why do you think Kavi was surprised by what his grandfather told him about empires?**
   - What did he expect empires to be like before he saw the maps?
2. **What are some of the goods that empires traded through their networks?**
   - Can you name at least three items and the regions they came from?
3. **Besides goods, what other things moved along trade routes?**
   - How might the movement of ideas or people affect societies?
4. **How did geography affect where and how trade happened?**
   - Why were certain cities or regions more powerful in trade?
5. **What role did technology (like ships or roads) play in helping empires grow?**
   - How do you think innovations changed the speed or safety of trade?
6. **How did trade routes and imperial control help shape the modern world?**
   - Can you think of foods, languages, or technologies in your life that came from somewhere far away?
7. **Kavi asked, "What would the world look like without those routes?"**
   - How would your daily life be different without global trade?
8. **What is the difference between people moving by choice and being forced to move?**
   - Why is it important to understand both sides of that history?

Lesson 5: Mapping Empires – Power, Trade & Technology in Global History

Topic: Global empires and their influence on trade, technology, and geography

STEM Focus: Mapping, data visualization, resource modeling, trade route analysis

Subjects: World History, Geography, Political Science, Economics

---

💬 Teacher Letter

Dear Educator,

In this lesson, students explore how empires throughout history shaped the flow of goods, people, and ideas. By analyzing historical maps, trade data, and resource distribution, learners can visualize the reach of imperial power and the global impacts of technology and geography.

This activity helps students think spatially and systematically—critical components of both historical thinking and STEM learning. Mapping trade routes and resource flows offers an authentic opportunity to apply data interpretation and modeling skills.

As students track the technological tools and infrastructure that enabled global empires to expand, they begin to see history not just as a story of conquest—but as a story of systems, networks, and human decisions that echo into our world today.

With respect,

Beverly Simmons

Author, Educator, Curriculum Developer

5E Lesson Plan: Mapping Empires – Power, Trade & Technology

Engage

Prompt:
Show a historical trade map (e.g., Silk Road, Trans-Saharan, British Imperial shipping lanes). Ask:

- What do you think these routes carried?
- Who controlled the routes? Who benefited?

Explore

Activity:
Students examine maps or tables showing:

- The size and reach of selected empires (e.g., Mongol, Roman, Ottoman, British)
- Trade routes and key resources (spices, silk, cotton, gold, oil)
- Technology that enabled empire expansion (ships, roads, communication systems)

Task:
Each group selects an empire, maps its reach, trade connections, and technologies. Then they model one global impact (e.g., spread of technology, disease, language, or resource control).

Explain

Mini-Lecture / Class Discussion:

- What do maps tell us about power and priorities in different time periods?
- How did geography and technology shape the success or failure of empires?
- What are the patterns across time (e.g., controlling choke points, resource zones)?

Extend

Project Options:

- Create an illustrated map with trade routes, power centers, and innovation points
- Build a cause-effect web showing one empire's global impact
- Model how a modern empire (corporate or digital) compares in structure and reach

STEM Focus:
Mapping, modeling, systems thinking, technology impact analysis

Evaluate

Assessment Options:

- Presentation of maps or models with student explanation
- Reflection essay: "What does mapping teach us about history?"
- Peer review of visual clarity and use of STEM skills

Rubric: Mapping Empires – Power, Trade & Technology

Grades 6–12 Rubric with Point Values (Total: 24 points)

Criteria	4 pts (Excellent)	3 pts (Proficient)	2 pts (Developing)	1 pt (Needs Improvement)
Historical Accuracy	Empire, trade routes, and technologies clearly accurate	Mostly accurate with minor errors	Some facts unclear or inconsistent	Limited or inaccurate historical details
Visual Mapping	Map is clear, labeled, and well-organized	Map mostly clear with a few missing elements	Hard to follow or lacks detail	Unclear or disorganized map
Use of Trade or Resource Data	Trade/resource patterns clearly shown and explained	Patterns shown but not fully explained	Limited use or unclear pattern	No use of trade/resource data
STEM Integration	Strong modeling or data visualization techniques used	Some STEM applied effectively	STEM use present but underdeveloped	Little or no STEM integration
Global Impact Analysis	Clear, insightful explanation of one global effect	Identifies effect with some explanation	Basic cause-effect shown	Effect unclear or unsupported
Communication & Clarity	Project is well-structured and easy to understand	Mostly clear; some weak spots	Hard to follow in places	Unclear or poorly presented

Scoring Guide:

22–24: Excellent

18–21: Proficient

14–17: Developing

Below 14: Needs Improvement

Teacher Comments:

Student Reflection: What did you learn about how empires used technology and geography to shape the world?

Simplified Rubric (Grades 3–5)

Total Possible: 12 points

Category	3 pts – Great Job	2 pts – Getting There	1 pt – Needs Work
Map Details	Map is neat and shows clear empire borders and trade paths	Some features missing or hard to read	Map is messy or incorrect
Facts About Empire	Good info about trade and technology	Some info correct	Little or no useful facts
Global Effect	Shows how empire affected the world	Idea shared but unclear	No effect shown
Neatness & Effort	Project is neat and shows care	Some care shown	Rushed or sloppy

Scoring Guide:

11–12: Great Job!

8–10: Keep Going!

4–7: Let's Improve It!

Student Handouts:
Mapping Empires – Power, Trade & Technology

Introduction:

Throughout history, empires rose and expanded based on their control of land, resources, and technology. This activity helps you explore how geography and innovation shaped trade routes and global influence.

Your Task:

1. Choose one empire from the list below.

2. Use historical data and maps to explore how it grew and traded.

3. Create a map that shows the empire's borders, trade routes, and key cities.

4. Model one global impact that this empire had on trade, technology, or culture.

Empire Options:

- Roman Empire

- Mongol Empire

- Ottoman Empire

- British Empire

- Mali Empire

- Chinese Empires (Han, Tang, Ming)

- Spanish Empire

Sample Trade Goods and Routes:

Good Traded	Region of Origin	Empires Involved
Silk	China	Han, Tang, Mongol, Roman (Silk Road)
Gold	West Africa	Mali, Portuguese, Ottoman
Spices	India/Southeast Asia	British, Dutch, Ottoman
Cotton Textiles	India	British, Mughal, Roman
Silver	South America	Spanish Empire, Ming China
Salt	North Africa	Mali, Arab traders, Roman

Mapping Prompt:

• Draw the boundaries of your empire and major trade routes (by land or sea).

• Label major cities, ports, or trading hubs.

• Indicate where key goods originated and where they were traded.

• Add a legend explaining your symbols.

Impact Modeling Prompt:

Choose one global effect your empire had:

• Spread of a technology (printing, ship design, navigation tools)

• Language or religion shared across regions

• Disease transmission

• Cultural blending (foods, ideas, fashion)

Represent this in a creative format: an infographic, flowchart, or illustrated cause-effect chain.

Reflection Questions:

1. How did trade and technology help empires expand?

2. What geographic features helped or hurt their growth?

3. What modern global systems remind you of these empires?

4. How can maps help us understand power and change?

Lesson 6: Data on the Move – Migration, Refugees & Global Impact

💼 "The Suitcase Under the Stairs"

A Story to Introduce Historical Migration and Its Ripple Effects

Nico had walked past the old suitcase a hundred times. It sat tucked beneath the stairs at his grandmother's house, half-covered by a faded blanket and a stack of old magazines.

One rainy Saturday, while looking for board games, Nico finally asked, "What's in that?"

His grandmother paused, then gave him a quiet smile. "That," she said, "is the reason we're here."

She pulled the suitcase into the light. The leather was cracked, the buckles rusted. She opened it carefully. Inside were two photos, a map with red pins, a cloth doll, and a folded bus ticket dated 1946.

"This was your great-grandfather's," she said. "He carried it when he left the South and moved north during the Great Migration."

Nico blinked. "Like... a vacation?"

"Far from it," she said. "He left because there were no good jobs, no safety, and no future for him down there. He boarded a train with a suitcase and hope."

Nico gently unfolded the map. There were dots scattered from Mississippi to Michigan. "These are all the places he lived while looking for work," his grandmother explained. "He picked fruit, laid bricks, even cleaned hotel rooms."

"But why didn't he just stay home?" Nico asked.

"Because home wasn't always welcoming. Back then, laws and racism kept people like him from voting, earning fair wages, or even walking safely down the street."

"So he moved," Nico whispered.

"And he wasn't alone," she said. "Millions moved—north, west, across oceans. Some fled war. Others chased dreams. Every one of them changed the place they left, and the place they arrived."

Nico looked at the photos—one of a young man in a suit with tired eyes, the other of a brick house with kids on the porch. "That's him?"

"That's what he built," she said. "A new life. For us."

At school the next week, Nico stood in front of a map of migration patterns and raised his hand. "I know why people move," he said. "They don't just carry bags—they carry their stories. And when they arrive, they change everything. Even if no one sees it at first."

🧳 Discussion Questions: Understanding Migration

1. **Why did Nico's great-grandfather leave his home in the South?**
   - What reasons did his grandmother give for why people migrated during the Great Migration?

2. **What items were in the suitcase, and why do you think they were important?**
   - What can we learn about someone's journey through the objects they carry?

3. **What challenges did Nico's great-grandfather face when moving to a new place?**
   - How might those challenges be similar or different for migrants today?

4. **What does Nico mean when he says, "They don't just carry bags—they carry their stories"?**
   - How can someone's journey impact their family, their new home, and the place they left?

5. **How does migration affect more than just the people who move?**
   - Think about jobs, culture, neighborhoods, and politics.

6. **Why is it important to look at data and maps when studying migration?**
   - How can numbers and patterns help us understand human stories better?

7. **If you had to leave your home suddenly, what would you pack in your suitcase—and why?**
   - What would tell your story?

Lesson 6: Data on the Move – Migration, Refugees & Global Impact

Topic: Human migration patterns, causes, and consequences across history

STEM Focus: Data interpretation, mapping, trend analysis, modeling population flow

Subjects: World History, Geography, Civics, Global Studies

♥ Teacher Letter

Dear Educator,

Migration has shaped civilizations, cultures, and economies for centuries. In this lesson, students explore key historical migration events using data and maps to understand both the human stories and the systemic ripple effects. From the Great Migration in the U.S. to global refugee crises, learners connect individual journeys to broader trends in labor, politics, and geography.

This project-based lesson builds both empathy and analytical thinking. Students apply STEM skills like data interpretation and mapping to model how people move, why they move, and what happens next. These are essential skills for 21st-century learners— helping them understand the world through both numbers and narratives.

Warmly,
Beverly Simmons
Author, Educator, Curriculum Developer

5E Lesson Plan: Data on the Move – Migration, Refugees & Global Impact

Engage

Prompt:
Ask students to think of a time when they or someone they know moved. Then show images or a short video of historical migrations (e.g., Irish immigration, Syrian refugees, the Great Migration). Ask:

- Why do people move?
- What changes when many people move at once?

Explore

Activity:
Students examine data sets or maps showing:

- One major migration (e.g., Atlantic slave trade, Irish famine migration, Great Migration, Partition of India, Syrian civil war)
- Push/pull factors (war, famine, opportunity, climate, etc.)
- Population impacts on sending and receiving regions

Task:
Students graph or model migration patterns, analyze population changes, and annotate maps to show human impact.

Explain

Discussion Points:

- What do the data and maps reveal about causes and effects?
- How does migration impact labor markets, urbanization, or conflict?
- How do STEM tools help tell migration stories beyond the headlines?

Extend

Project Ideas:

- Create a visual model (e.g., flowchart or infographic) showing a migration chain
- Use real or simulated data to predict outcomes of forced migration (e.g., refugee settlement planning)
- Design a "Migration News Report" that presents both personal and statistical perspectives

STEM Focus:
Population modeling, mapping, graphing, trend analysis

Evaluate

Assessment Options:

- Migration model or map with explanation of findings
- Short reflection or script explaining a migration event from two perspectives
- Peer review and gallery walk of migration visual projects

Rubric: Data on the Move – Migration, Refugees & Global Impact

Grades 6–12 Rubric with Point Values (Total: 24 points)

Criteria	4 pts (Excellent)	3 pts (Proficient)	2 pts (Developing)	1 pt (Needs Improvement)
Historical Understanding	Migration event and context clearly and accurately explained	Mostly accurate with minor errors	Some understanding, lacking clarity	Inaccurate or missing context
Data Use & Analysis	Data clearly supports findings and insights	Data used appropriately with basic insight	Limited or partially correct data use	Data is unclear or misused
Map or Visual Model	Visual is clear, accurate, and well-labeled	Mostly clear with some missing parts	Basic visual; lacks clarity	Poorly done or incomplete visual
Global Impact Explanation	Clearly explains how migration affected people and places	Impact noted with general explanation	Some impact mentioned, lacks depth	Little or no explanation of impact
STEM Integration	Strong use of mapping, graphing, or modeling	STEM techniques present and mostly clear	STEM elements weak or confusing	No STEM techniques shown
Communication & Presentation	Work is clear, organized, and insightful	Mostly well-presented with a few flaws	Basic presentation lacking detail	Unclear or hard to follow

Scoring Guide:

22–24: Excellent

18–21: Proficient

14–17: Developing

Below 14: Needs Improvement

Teacher Comments:

Student Reflection: What can data and stories teach us about the causes and consequences of migration?

Simplified Rubric (Grades 3–5)

Total Possible: 12 points

Category	3 pts – Great Job	2 pts – Getting There	1 pt – Needs Work
Story of Movement	Migration reason and story are clear	Basic story with some errors	Story is missing or unclear
Map or Visual	Map or chart is easy to understand	Some parts hard to follow	Very messy or confusing
Effect on Places	Explains how places changed	Basic idea shared	Little or no impact shown
Neatness & Effort	Neat and complete	Some parts unfinished	Messy or rushed

Scoring Guide:

11–12: Great Job!   8–10: Keep Going!   4–7: Let's Improve It!

Student Handouts: Data on the Move – Migration, Refugees & Global Impact

Introduction:

People move for many reasons—some by choice, others by force. This activity helps you explore major human migrations, analyze causes and effects, and use data and maps to tell migration stories in a visual and meaningful way.

Your Task:

1. Choose a major migration from the list below.

2. Use maps, population data, and historical context to understand why it happened and what changed.

3. Create a map, graph, or visual model showing the migration.

4. Reflect on how migration shapes communities and the world.

Migration Event Examples:

- Atlantic Slave Trade

- Great Migration (African Americans in the U.S.)

- Irish Famine Migration

- Partition of India (1947)

- Syrian Refugee Crisis

- Venezuelan Migration (21st century)

- Rohingya Crisis

- Dust Bowl Migration (U.S.)

Sample Migration Data (Excerpt):

Migration Event	Time Period	Push Factors	Estimated People Moved
Atlantic Slave Trade	1500–1800s	Enslavement, forced labor	12–15 million
Irish Famine	1845–1852	Starvation, poverty	Over 1 million
Partition of India	1947	Religious conflict, violence	14–16 million
Great Migration	1916–1970	Racism, lack of jobs in South	6 million
Syrian Crisis	2011–present	War, persecution	6.6 million refugees
Dust Bowl Migration	1930s	Environmental disaster, economic hardship	2.5 million

Mapping & Modeling Prompt:

• Create a map that shows where people left and where they went.

• Label key countries, cities, or regions involved.

• Use arrows or color codes to show direction and flow.

• Create a graph or flowchart explaining the causes and effects of the migration.

• Optional: Add a personal story or quote from a migrant to humanize the data.

Reflection Questions:

1. What do you think is the hardest part of migrating?

2. How can data and stories help us understand migration better?

3. What changes in the places people leave and the places they go?

4. Can you think of ways your community has been shaped by migration?

Lesson 7: War by the Numbers – Analyzing Conflict Through Data

$ "Counting the Cost"

A Story to Introduce War, Numbers, and the Big Questions Behind Conflict

The question came out of nowhere, right in the middle of math class.

"Why do we spend so much on war?" asked Mateo.

The room went quiet. Their teacher, Mr. Ross, paused before answering. "That's a big question, Mateo. One we're going to explore together."

That afternoon, Mr. Ross wheeled in a tall stack of posters and charts. One showed the U.S. defense budget. Another listed the number of lives lost in major wars: World War I, World War II, Vietnam, Iraq.

"There's something numbers can do that stories alone can't," Mr. Ross explained. "They show scale. They help us see how big something really is."

He pointed to a bar graph that stretched across the board. "This," he said, "is how much the U.S. spends on its military every year. And these—" he pointed to smaller bars, "—are budgets for education, science, and health."

Mateo leaned forward. "Why is the war one so tall?"

"Because war is expensive," Mr. Ross said. "Not just in money, but in lives. Look at this chart."

The next graph showed millions of small figures—some shaded in red. Each red one represented someone lost in a major war. "These aren't just numbers," Mr. Ross said quietly. "These are parents, friends, children. Every dot is a life."

The class stared. The chart stretched so wide it covered two walls.

"But why does it keep happening?" asked Jayla.

"Because sometimes people think war is the only solution," Mr. Ross said. "But history shows us it's usually the last resort—and sometimes, the result of bad planning, bad math, or bad priorities."

He handed out a worksheet. It wasn't about memorizing battle names. It was a budget breakdown—military vs. infrastructure, past spending vs. present, projected costs vs. potential savings.

"Your job," he said, "is to be the Congress of Tomorrow. Look at this data. Ask questions. Make decisions. Because the more we understand the cost of conflict, the better we can work for peace."

Mateo raised his hand again. "Can math really stop a war?"

Mr. Ross smiled. "Math can ask the right questions. And sometimes, asking the right questions changes everything."

📚 Books Written During or About War-Time Experiences

1. The Diary of Anne Frank **by Anne Frank**

- *World War II (Holocaust)*
- A powerful first-person account of a Jewish girl hiding with her family in Nazi-occupied Amsterdam.
- **Why it matters:** Shows the human cost of war and persecution from a child's perspective.

2. Night **by Elie Wiesel**

- *World War II (Holocaust)*
- A memoir of surviving Auschwitz, written with haunting honesty.
- **Why it matters:** Connects personal suffering to broader consequences of war and hatred.

3. Farewell to Manzanar **by Jeanne Wakatsuki Houston & James D. Houston**

- *World War II (Japanese Internment Camps in the U.S.)*

- A family's experience being forcibly relocated during wartime paranoia.
- **Why it matters**: Explores how war can impact citizens' rights and justice at home.

4. Zlata's Diary **by Zlata Filipović**

- *Bosnian War (1990s)*
- Often called the "Anne Frank of Sarajevo," this diary captures a child's life in a war-torn city.
- **Why it matters**: Highlights how war disrupts everyday life—and how kids are affected.

5. Soldier's Heart **by Gary Paulsen**

- *U.S. Civil War (fiction based on fact)*
- Follows a young soldier's emotional journey and trauma during the Civil War.
- **Why it matters**: Explores the mental and physical toll of war on young people.

6. They Called Us Enemy **by George Takei**

- *World War II (Japanese-American internment, graphic memoir)*
- Star Trek actor George Takei tells his family's story of being placed in an internment camp as a child.
- **Why it matters**: Combines history, identity, and personal memory in an accessible format.

7. When My Name Was Keoko **by Linda Sue Park**

- *World War II (Japanese occupation of Korea, historical fiction)*
- A brother and sister navigate war and cultural oppression in 1940s Korea.
- **Why it matters**: Brings attention to under-taught global impacts of war.

Art of STEM

Lesson 7: War by the Numbers – Analyzing Conflict Through Data

Topic: Major wars in history, their causes, consequences, and data-driven impact

STEM Focus: Data analysis, casualty comparison, economic modeling, systems thinking

Subjects: U.S. History, World History, Civics, Political Science

---

♥ Teacher Letter

Dear Educator,

This lesson helps students explore history's most devastating wars not just through stories and dates, but through numbers that reveal the scope and human cost of conflict. By comparing data on casualties, alliances, and economic impacts, students develop a deeper understanding of the systems that drive wars—and the toll they take on societies.

STEM skills like data interpretation, graphing, and cause-effect modeling are crucial for understanding complex historical events. Students learn to make sense of the past by identifying patterns, calculating impacts, and visualizing decisions in times of conflict.

This approach fosters not only analytical thinking, but also empathy and global awareness—key goals for any classroom preparing students for the future.

Sincerely,

Beverly Simmons

Author, Educator, Curriculum Developer

5E Lesson Plan: War by the Numbers – Analyzing Conflict Through Data

Engage

Prompt:
Display two sets of numbers from different wars (e.g., WWII vs. Vietnam): casualties, duration, cost, number of countries involved. Ask students:

- Which war seems "bigger"? Why?
- What do numbers tell us that stories might not?

Explore

Activity:
Students work with data sets showing:

- Major wars (e.g., Revolutionary War, Civil War, WWI, WWII, Vietnam, Iraq)
- Casualties, economic cost, duration, countries involved
- Civilian vs. military deaths, long-term impacts

Task:
Create graphs or infographics comparing two wars. Interpret patterns. Model the impact of one aspect of war (e.g., war spending, alliances, reconstruction, or displacement).

Explain

Mini-Lesson or Group Discussion:

- How does analyzing data help us understand the scale and impact of war?
- What do graphs reveal about changes in warfare over time?
- How might decisions have changed if leaders had different data?

Extend

Project Options:

- Create a war profile infographic (visual summary of one war)
- Write a policy recommendation as a historical advisor using data trends
- Model alternative outcomes if a war decision had changed (e.g., what if peace talks succeeded?)

STEM Focus:
Graphing, modeling, trend analysis, economic calculations

Evaluate

Assessment Options:

- Presentation or infographic with data citations
- Short reflection essay connecting human and data perspectives
- Peer review of clarity, insight, and use of evidence

Rubric: War by the Numbers – Analyzing Conflict Through Data

Grades 6–12 Rubric with Point Values (Total: 24 points)

Criteria	4 pts (Excellent)	3 pts (Proficient)	2 pts (Developing)	1 pt (Needs Improvement)
Historical Accuracy	War context and data accurately presented	Mostly accurate with few errors	Some information unclear or inconsistent	Inaccurate or missing details
Data Visualization	Graphs or visuals are clear, labeled, and meaningful	Mostly clear visuals with minor errors	Hard to read or limited visuals	Unclear or missing visual elements
Comparative Analysis	Insightful comparison of conflicts and patterns	Some comparison with basic insight	Limited or surface-level comparison	No real comparison shown
STEM Integration	Data calculations, modeling, and systems thinking are strong	Some STEM skills applied effectively	STEM use is minimal or weak	No STEM skills demonstrated
Global or Human Impact	Clear explanation of war's effects on people/societies	Some effects noted	Basic or unclear description of effects	No effect or explanation shown
Presentation & Clarity	Well-structured and easy to follow	Mostly clear with minor issues	Hard to follow at times	Unclear or poorly organized

Scoring Guide:

22–24: Excellent

18–21: Proficient

14–17: Developing

Below 14: Needs Improvement

Teacher Comments:

Student Reflection: What did the numbers and graphs reveal about war that stories alone do not?

Simplified Rubric (Grades 3–5)

Total Possible: 12 points

Category	3 pts – Great Job	2 pts – Getting There	1 pt – Needs Work
Facts About the War	Includes accurate facts and numbers	Some facts included	Missing or incorrect info
Graph or Chart	Clear and labeled graph or visual	Some parts unclear or missing	Visual is hard to follow
War Impact	Explains how war affected people	Some explanation	Little or no impact explained
Neatness & Effort	Neat and thoughtful work	Some effort shown	Rushed or messy

Scoring Guide:

11–12: Great Job!

8–10: Keep Going!

4–7: Let's Improve It!

Student Handouts: War by the Numbers – Analyzing Conflict Through Data

Introduction:

Wars have shaped human history, but they are more than just battles and leaders. This activity uses numbers—like casualty counts, durations, and costs—to understand the scope and consequences of major conflicts.

Your Task:

1. Choose one or two wars from the list below.

2. Use provided data to explore and compare the impacts.

3. Create a graph, infographic, or visual model that tells the story of these conflicts through numbers.

4. Reflect on how data reveals patterns and human impact in war.

Sample Conflicts to Explore:

- American Revolutionary War

- U.S. Civil War

- World War I

- World War II

- Vietnam War

- Iraq War (2003–2011)

- Russia–Ukraine War (ongoing)

- Global Conflicts (for comparison)

Sample War Data:

War	Years	Casualties (Est.)	Countries Involved	Estimated Cost (USD)
American Revolutionary War	1775–1783	25,000+	2	$2.4 billion (modern USD)
U.S. Civil War	1861–1865	750,000+	1 (internal)	$5.2 billion (1860s USD)
World War I	1914–1918	20 million+	30+	$208 billion
World War II	1939–1945	70–85 million	50+	$1.6 trillion
Vietnam War	1955–1975	3 million+	5+	$168 billion
Iraq War	2003–2011	500,000+	12+	$2.4 trillion

Data Visualization & Analysis:

• Choose a chart type (bar, line, pie, flow map) to represent your war data.

• Include titles, labels, and sources.

• Annotate your visual with insights (e.g., 'This war caused the highest number of civilian deaths.')

Systems Modeling Prompt:

Pick one system affected by the war (e.g., economy, population, healthcare, environment) and create a cause-and-effect model showing:

- What changed and why

- Short- and long-term impacts

- Possible alternatives or consequences if history changed

Reflection Questions:

1. How did the wars you studied differ in terms of human cost and global reach?

2. What surprised you most when looking at the numbers?

3. How can understanding war through data help us make better decisions in the future?

4. What would you want future generations to understand from these visuals?

Lesson 8: Building a Nation – Infrastructure, Innovation & Inequality

Lesson 8: Building a Nation – Infrastructure, Innovation & Inequality

Topic: The development of infrastructure in shaping nations and economies

STEM Focus: Engineering systems, transportation mapping, cost modeling, data analysis

Subjects: U.S. History, Civics, Geography, Economics

💜 Teacher Letter

Dear Educator,

The bridges we cross, roads we travel, and technologies we depend on didn't just appear—they were built, often with ambition and conflict hand in hand. In this lesson, students explore how infrastructure projects shaped national identity, spurred innovation, and sometimes deepened inequalities.

Students investigate projects like the Transcontinental Railroad, the Interstate Highway System, or rural electrification using real-world STEM skills: cost analysis, systems modeling, and map-based planning. By examining who benefited, who was displaced, and what innovation required, students understand how building a nation is both a technical and moral act.

This lesson brings engineering and equity together through a social studies lens—making STEM relevant and purposeful in the history classroom.

In service of future-ready learners,
Beverly Simmons
Author, Educator, Curriculum Developer

🌉 "The Bridge Between Us"

A.Story.to.Introduce.the.Power.of.Infrastructure

It started with a drawing.

Maria had been staring at the river her whole life. It cut through her city like a ribbon—beautiful, winding, and inconvenient. Her grandma lived on the other side, and every visit meant a long bus ride looping around the only bridge for miles.

"If I built a bridge here," Maria whispered one day, sketching lines in her notebook, "it would take five minutes instead of fifty."

Her teacher saw the sketch and smiled. "That's how it always starts—with an idea and a reason to connect."

Soon, Maria's class was learning about bridges, tunnels, roads, and train lines—how they weren't just built for convenience, but to shape how people lived, worked, and moved.

They studied the transcontinental railroad, the interstate highway system, even canals dug with shovels and sweat. Some projects brought towns together. Others split them apart.

Maria was shocked. "You mean some bridges were built for only *some* people?"

Her teacher nodded. "Infrastructure can connect—but it can also divide. That's why it matters who designs it... and why."

In a classroom debate, students posed tough questions:
Should a highway go through a park or around it?
How do you balance speed with safety?
What if a neighborhood is left behind?

Maria thought about her grandma. About the kids on the other side of the river who couldn't get to the new library easily.

That weekend, she showed her sketch to the city engineer visiting their school's career fair. He looked at it carefully, then said, "You've thought this through. You even marked where the supports go. Ever think about becoming an engineer?"

Maria lit up. "I just want to build something that helps everyone."

The engineer nodded. "That's exactly what we need more of."

Years later, long after Maria had grown up and earned her degree, a new pedestrian bridge opened in her old neighborhood. It arched over the river like a handshake. At the ribbon cutting, Maria stood beside her grandmother.

"This bridge," the mayor said, "connects more than just roads. It connects people, possibilities—and hope."

Maria smiled as children ran across it, bikes zipping by. She whispered, "It started with a drawing."

🧠 Reflection Questions

Why did Maria want to build a bridge in the first place?

What problem was she trying to solve?

What are some ways infrastructure can connect people?

Can you think of examples from your own town or city?

How can infrastructure also divide or hurt communities?

What kinds of questions should planners ask before they build?

What does Maria mean when she says, "I just want to build something that helps everyone"?

Why is it important for public projects to include all people?

What did you learn about how bridges and roads shape our lives beyond just travel?

🔨 Classroom Design Challenge: Build to Connect

Prompt: Imagine your town or city is building something new to bring people together—like a bridge, park, library, or public transit stop. Your job is to design it in a way that connects, includes, and inspires.

Steps:

Pick a Purpose:

What problem are you solving? (e.g., long travel times, unsafe paths, lack of green space)

Plan Your People:

Who will use it? Think about kids, elders, people with disabilities, and families.

Sketch It Out:

Use paper or digital tools to draw your design. Label features like ramps, signs, or safe zones.

Add Data:

Show the benefits with numbers! How many people would use it? How much time would it save?

Share & Reflect:

Present your design to the class. How does your project connect people? What challenges did you solve?

5E Lesson Plan: Building a Nation – Infrastructure, Innovation & Inequality

Engage

Prompt:
Show images of major U.S. infrastructure (e.g., Hoover Dam, Panama Canal, railroads, broadband internet expansion). Ask:

- What do you think it took to build these?
- Who benefits most from these systems?

Explore

Activity:
Students explore historical infrastructure projects through maps, timelines, cost records, and population data. Choose one:

- Transcontinental Railroad
- Erie Canal
- Hoover Dam
- Interstate Highway System
- Tennessee Valley Authority (TVA)
- Broadband/Internet expansion (modern)

Task:
Create a system model: who built it, what it cost, who was affected (positively or negatively), and what changed.

Explain

Discussion Points:

- What were the goals of this project?
- What systems were involved (labor, materials, government, environment)?
- How do we know if an infrastructure project was "successful"?

Extend

Project Options:

- Create a visual model of the project's system: inputs, outputs, stakeholders, outcomes
- Design a plan for a future infrastructure project your community needs
- Research how technology (like AI or drones) might change infrastructure today

STEM Focus:
Engineering systems, mapping, modeling, cost-benefit analysis, impact modeling

---

Evaluate

Assessment Options:

- Annotated diagram or system model with a written explanation
- Group presentation: "Build This!" proposal for modern infrastructure
- Personal reflection: "Who builds progress—and who gets left behind?"

Infrastructure Project Analysis Rubric

Total Points: ___ / 100
Note: This rubric can be used for both the system model creation and the "Build This!" proposal activities outlined in the lesson plan.

Category	Exceptional (25-20)	Proficient (19-15)	Developing (14-10)	Beginning (9-0)
Project Development and Research	Thorough research of historical infrastructure project with comprehensive data collection on costs, timeline, and impact	Good research with most key data points included	Basic research with some missing key information	Limited research with significant gaps in information
Systems Analysis	Clear identification of all systems involved (labor, materials, government, environmental) with detailed connections	Most systems identified with basic connections explained	Some systems identified but connections unclear	Few systems identified with minimal explanation
Impact Assessment	Comprehensive analysis of both positive and negative impacts on different stakeholders	Good analysis of major impacts with some stakeholder perspectives	Basic analysis of impacts with limited stakeholder perspectives	Minimal analysis of impacts with one-sided perspective
Presentation and Communication	Clear, organized presentation with effective use of visuals and technical vocabulary	Organized presentation with some visual supports and appropriate vocabulary	Basic presentation with limited visual supports or technical vocabulary	Unclear presentation lacking visual supports or appropriate vocabulary

Scoring Guide:

11–12: Great Job!

8–10: Keep Going!

4–7: Let's Improve It!

Building America: Infrastructure Explorer Activities

Activity 1: Infrastructure Investigation Worksheet

Project Analysis

Choose one of the following infrastructure projects to research and analyze:

- Transcontinental Railroad
- Erie Canal
- Hoover Dam
- Interstate Highway System
- Tennessee Valley Authority (TVA)
- Modern Broadband Expansion

Part A: Project Facts

1. Name of Project: _____
2. Years of Construction: _
3. Total Cost (at the time): _
4. Location(s): _____
5. Main Purpose: _____

Part B: System Mapping

Draw or chart the following elements of your infrastructure project:

- Materials needed
- Workers involved
- Communities affected
- Environmental impacts
- Economic outcomes

Part C: Impact Analysis

1. Who benefited from this project? List at least 3 groups:
   - _____
   - _____
   - _____

2. Who was negatively affected? List at least 2 groups:
   - _____

Activity 2: Modern Infrastructure Design Challenge

Your Community's Future

1. Identify an infrastructure need in your community
2. Create a proposal including:
   - Project description
   - Estimated cost
   - Timeline
   - Benefits to community
   - Potential challenges
   - Environmental considerations

Cost Analysis Table

Complete this table for your proposed project:

Item	Estimated Cost
Materials	
Labor	
Equipment	
Planning	
Total	

Activity 3: Technology and Infrastructure Worksheet

Future Technologies

Research how these technologies might change infrastructure:

1. Artificial Intelligence

   - Current use: ____

   - Future potential: __

2. Drones

   - Current use: ____

   - Future potential: __

3. Renewable Energy

   - Current use: ____

   - Future potential: __

Reflection Questions

1. How might these technologies make infrastructure projects more efficient?

2. What new challenges might these technologies create?

3. How can we ensure new infrastructure benefits everyone in the community?

Note: These activities align with 8th-grade standards in social studies, geography, and STEM, encouraging critical thinking about infrastructure development while maintaining age-appropriate complexity levels.

Art STEM

Lesson 9: Hidden Figures – Representation, Recognition & STEM Gaps

"The Name in the Margin"

A Story to Introduce Hidden Contributors in STEM

It started with a math problem.

A hard one.

Leila tapped her pencil against her notebook, staring at a page full of calculations. It was a practice question for their school's STEM fair, but no matter how she rearranged the numbers, she couldn't get the rocket's arc to land in the right spot.

Frustrated, she flipped her textbook shut—and that's when she noticed it.

In tiny letters, along the bottom edge of the back cover, was a name she didn't recognize: **C. Johnson**

"Who's that?" she asked her teacher.

Mr. Nguyen smiled. "Ah. That's Katherine Johnson. You might've seen her in the movie *Hidden Figures*."

Leila blinked. "She was a real person?"

"Oh, very real," he said. "She helped NASA calculate the exact trajectories needed to send astronauts into space and bring them home safely. She was brilliant—one of the best minds of her time."

Leila flipped back through the book. There were chapters about Newton, Galileo, Einstein. But no Johnson. No C. Johnson anywhere in the pages.

"She's not in here," Leila said.

Mr. Nguyen nodded. "That's the thing about history. Sometimes the people who do the most important work are the ones we hear about the least."

That night, Leila dove into research. She read about Katherine Johnson, Dorothy Vaughan, and Mary Jackson—Black women whose calculations were behind the success of space missions but whose names were buried for decades.

She also found doctors, engineers, inventors—people who never made it into the spotlight, but made everything else possible.

It hit her like a falling star: the missing names didn't mean their work wasn't there. It meant people had just stopped looking.

The next day at the STEM fair, Leila presented a simple rocket simulation. But next to her model, she placed a chart.

It showed names of historical STEM leaders on one side—and a blank space next to each for contributors who had worked behind the scenes.

The judges were intrigued.

"Why the blanks?" one asked.

Leila smiled. "Because history's still catching up. And I think we should start filling in the margins."

🔍 Activity: Fill in the Margins—Uncovering Hidden STEM Figures

Objective:
Students will research lesser-known innovators—especially women, people of color, and marginalized individuals—in STEM fields, and create a class display that highlights their contributions.

Step 1: Investigate the Gaps

Discuss:

Who usually shows up in your textbooks or history lessons when it comes to science, technology, engineering, or math?

Who *doesn't* you see?

Why might some people be "in the margins" of history?

Step 2: Research a Hidden Figure

Each student selects or is assigned a lesser-known STEM contributor. They can choose from a curated list (see examples below) or discover someone new.

Possible Hidden Figures:

Katherine Johnson (NASA mathematician)

Dr. Chien-Shiung Wu (nuclear physicist)

Dr. Charles Drew (pioneer of blood banking)

Mary Golda Ross (first Native American female engineer)

Gladys West (helped develop GPS)

Mark Dean (co-inventor of the PC)

Ellen Ochoa (first Hispanic woman in space)

Step 3: Create a "History Margin Card"

On a small poster or digital slide, each student includes:
- ☑ Name
- ☑ Field of work
- ☑ A short description of their contribution
- ☑ A visual (photo, drawing, or symbol of their work)
- ☑ A quote (if available) or something meaningful the student learned

Step 4: Build a Wall of Names

Display the students' Margin Cards around the classroom or in a hallway under a banner:
"STEM: Filling In the Margins of History"

Optional: Create a timeline or "invisible history" collage to show when and where these figures made their impact.

Reflection Questions (Optional Exit Ticket):

Why do you think some people were left out of mainstream history?

What might we miss if we only tell part of the story?

How can we make sure more voices are included in the future?

Lesson 9: Hidden Figures – Representation, Recognition & STEM Gaps

Art of STEM

Topic: Underrepresented individuals and groups in history who contributed to science, math, and engineering

STEM Focus: Data analysis, representation metrics, equity modeling, communication

Subjects: U.S. History, World History, Civics, Math, Career Exploration

---

💜 Teacher Letter

Dear Educator,

This lesson invites students to uncover and analyze the hidden contributions of individuals often left out of mainstream narratives—especially women, people of color, and marginalized innovators in STEM. By using data to examine who is represented in history books, awards, and leadership, students confront the relationship between power, visibility, and access.

Through research and data projects, students engage in both historical recovery and mathematical reasoning. They explore gaps in recognition, analyze representation trends, and model how equity can be measured—and changed.

By connecting historical inquiry to social justice and STEM inclusion, this lesson helps students understand that the future of innovation depends on the voices we choose to include.

With purpose and pride,
Beverly Simmons
Author, Educator, Curriculum Developer

5E Lesson Plan: Hidden Figures – Representation, Recognition & STEM Gaps

Engage

Prompt:
Show images of famous inventors and scientists (e.g., Einstein, Edison, Newton). Ask:

- Who do you recognize?
- Who's missing from this picture?
- Why do you think some names are better known than others?

Explore

Activity:
Students research lesser-known historical figures in STEM (e.g., Katherine Johnson, Mary Jackson, Mae Jemison, Benjamin Banneker, Ada Lovelace, Ellen Ochoa).
They collect data about representation across eras and compare to current STEM workforce diversity stats.

Task:

- Build a profile or infographic of one historical figure
- Analyze representation data (e.g., % of women/minorities in STEM by decade)
- Model what representation could look like with equity policies in place

Explain

Discussion Topics:

- What patterns do you see in representation over time?
- What helped or hindered recognition?
- Why does visibility matter in STEM and in history?

Extend

Project Options:

- Create a timeline or visual gallery of underrecognized STEM figures
- Write a recommendation for improving diversity in a specific STEM field
- Design a museum exhibit featuring Hidden Figures of STEM

STEM Focus:
Data analysis, equity modeling, mathematical reasoning, visual design

---

Evaluate

Assessment Options:

- Personal reflection: "Whose story needs to be told?"
- Group project: Representation dashboard or timeline
- Written or visual comparison: past vs. present STEM demographics

Rubric: Hidden Figures – Representation, Recognition & STEM Gaps

Grades 6–12 Rubric with Point Values (Total: 24 points)

Criteria	4 pts (Excellent)	3 pts (Proficient)	2 pts (Developing)	1 pt (Needs Improvement)
Historical Research	Detailed and accurate profile of underrepresented figure(s)	Good research with minor gaps	Basic summary or some inaccuracies	Incomplete or unclear information
Data Interpretation	Clear analysis of representation data over time	Basic interpretation with some clarity	Limited or unclear interpretation	Minimal or no use of data
Equity Modeling	Insightful model of gaps and equity improvements	Solid effort with some innovation	Basic or vague equity model	Missing or off-topic model
Creativity & Design	Infographic/timeline is engaging and well-designed	Mostly clear and well-structured	Some design flaws or missing pieces	Unclear or hard to follow
Critical Thinking	Strong insight into historical patterns and impacts	Some deeper thought shown	Surface-level explanation	Little or no critical thinking evident
Presentation & Reflection	Work is clear, reflective, and polished	Mostly complete and thoughtful	Somewhat disorganized	Messy or lacks depth

Scoring Guide:

22–24: Excellent

18–21: Proficient

14–17: Developing

Below 14: Needs Improvement

Teacher Comments:

Student Reflection: Whose story inspired you most, and why do you think they were hidden from history?

Simplified Rubric (Grades 3–5)

Total Possible: 12 points

Category	3 pts – Great Job	2 pts – Getting There	1 pt – Needs Work
STEM Hero	Shared who they were and what they did	Some information shared	Missing or incorrect info
Data Chart or Drawing	Used data or a good visual	Basic chart or unclear drawing	Missing or confusing visual
Fairness Message	Explains why their work matters	Some reflection shown	Hard to tell what student learned
Effort & Neatness	Work is neat and shows care	Some effort shown	Messy or rushed

Scoring Guide:

11–12: Great Job!

8–10: Keep Going!

4–7: Let's Improve It!

Student Handouts: Hidden Figures – Representation, Recognition & STEM Gaps

Introduction:

Throughout history, many people made important contributions to science, math, and engineering—but were left out of textbooks and awards. In this activity, you'll explore one of these 'hidden figures' and use data to better understand gaps in representation.

Your Task:

1. Choose a STEM innovator from the list or find your own.

2. Research what they contributed and what barriers they faced.

3. Explore STEM workforce data and compare past vs. present.

4. Create a timeline, infographic, or model showing how equity has changed—or could improve in the future.

Figure Options:

- Katherine Johnson (NASA mathematician)

- Benjamin Banneker (astronomer, surveyor)

- Ada Lovelace (early computer programmer)

- Mary Jackson (aerospace engineer)

- Ellen Ochoa (first Latina astronaut)

- Mae Jemison (physician, engineer, astronaut)

- Other underrepresented contributors of your choice

Representation Data Activity:

Use the sample data below or research your own:

- In 1980, women made up 8% of STEM jobs in the U.S.

- In 2020, women held 27% of STEM jobs

- In 1990, Black and Hispanic workers made up 12% of STEM fields combined

- In 2021, they made up 16% of STEM fields

Create a chart comparing decades. What's improved? What still needs work?

Equity Modeling Prompt:

Design a diagram that shows how one of the following systems affects STEM equity:

- School access or tracking

- Representation in textbooks/media

- Mentorship and role models

- Hiring and promotion in STEM careers

Include inputs (barriers/supports), outcomes, and ideas to close the gap.

Reflection Questions:

1. Why do you think some contributors were left out of the spotlight?

2. What kind of systems kept some people out of STEM fields?

3. What would more representation change—for individuals and society?

4. How can you help make sure stories like this are heard and remembered?

Lesson 10: The STEM Behind the Speeches – Analyzing Rhetoric, Statistics & Strategy

"The Speech That Changed Everything"

A Story to Introduce the Power of Persuasive Speech and Data

Ava had never spoken in front of a crowd before. Her heart pounded like a drum in her chest as she stood behind the podium in the school auditorium, gripping her notecards so tightly they wrinkled.

The gym was full. Students, teachers—even the mayor had come to hear the finalists of the "Voices for Change" contest.

Her project? *"Why Our City Needs More Green Space."*

She wasn't the loudest student. Or the most confident. But she was prepared.

Ava took a deep breath and began—not with a shout, but with a **statistic**.

"According to our city's planning report, less than 10% of our public land is used for parks and gardens. That's half the national average."

The room got quieter. People listened. Not because she was yelling—but because she had proof.

Next, she told a **story**: how her little brother wheezed from asthma attacks more often on weeks when they couldn't play outside, when the air near their apartment grew thick from traffic and smoke.

Then she used **logic**:

"More green space means cooler neighborhoods, cleaner air, and healthier people. Cities with more trees spend less on healthcare and energy. We invest once—and we save for years."

She ended with a call to action:

"Let's plant the future. Not just talk about it. Let's build a city where everyone can breathe."

The room burst into applause.

Later that night, Ava watched clips of famous speeches online: Lincoln at Gettysburg. Martin Luther King Jr. on the steps of the Lincoln Memorial. Malala Yousafzai at the UN, demanding education for girls.

Each speech was different. Some were poetic. Some were simple. But all of them shared the same tools: **structure, evidence, and courage**.

That's when Ava realized something:
Great speeches aren't just about what you say. They're about **why** you say it—and **how** you make people believe.

🗣 Build a Powerful Speech: Student Structure Guide

Title of Your Speech: _____

Topic or Issue: _____

◆ 1. Hook the Audience

Start with a question, fact, quote, or story that grabs attention.

Examples:
– "Did you know our city has fewer trees per person than almost any other in the country?"
– "When my grandmother fell on a broken sidewalk, I knew something had to change."

Your Hook:

_____

_____

_____

◆ 2. Present Your Claim (Main Argument)

What do you believe? What needs to change?

Example:
– "We must increase public funding for safe, green parks."

Your Claim:

_____

_____

_____

◆ 3. Use Evidence and Data

Support your claim with facts, statistics, or real-world examples.

Example:
– "According to the National Health Report, neighborhoods with more green space have 20% lower asthma rates."

Your Evidence:

◆ 4. Connect with Emotion

Tell a personal story or describe how the issue affects real people.

Example:
– "My younger brother can't safely play outside because there's no park within walking distance."

Your Story or Connection:

◆ 5. Offer a Solution

What do you want your audience to do? Think? Change? Support?

Example:
– "Let's pass the proposal for the new Riverside Park and fund it through the Green City Grant."

Your Solution or Call to Action:

◆ 6. Finish Strong

End with a bold statement, a hopeful vision, or a memorable quote.

Example:
– "Let's not wait. Let's grow something that lasts."

Your Closing Line:

Art of STEM

Lesson 10: The STEM Behind the Speeches – Analyzing Rhetoric, Statistics & Strategy

Topic: Famous speeches in U.S. and global history that use data, logic, and rhetorical strategy to persuade

STEM Focus: Data interpretation, logical reasoning, public communication, modeling cause-effect

Subjects: Civics, U.S. History, World History, English/ELA

♥ Teacher Letter

Dear Educator,

Speeches have shaped history—not just through emotion, but through reason, logic, and even science. This lesson helps students explore the role of data and structure in persuasive public speech. From Lincoln's Gettysburg Address to Malala's UN speech, students analyze how statistics, structure, and logical appeals are used to drive movements.

This approach invites students to dissect historical texts like engineers of language, using STEM lenses to decode their power. They don't just analyze persuasive elements—they measure them, model impact, and create their own.

It's a natural fit for interdisciplinary classrooms, encouraging students to become more thoughtful speakers, listeners, and decision-makers in a world shaped by data and discourse.

Warmly,
Beverly Simmons
Author, Educator, Curriculum Developer

"The Speech That Changed Everything"

A Story to Introduce the Power of Persuasive Speech and Data

Ava had never spoken in front of a crowd before. Her heart pounded like a drum in her chest as she stood behind the podium in the school auditorium, gripping her notecards so tightly they wrinkled.

The gym was full. Students, teachers—even the mayor had come to hear the finalists of the "Voices for Change" contest.

Her project? *"Why Our City Needs More Green Space."*

She wasn't the loudest student. Or the most confident. But she was prepared.

Ava took a deep breath and began—not with a shout, but with a **statistic**.

"According to our city's planning report, less than 10% of our public land is used for parks and gardens. That's half the national average."

The room got quieter. People listened. Not because she was yelling—but because she had proof.

Next, she told a **story**: how her little brother wheezed from asthma attacks more often on weeks when they couldn't play outside, when the air near their apartment grew thick from traffic and smoke.

Then she used **logic**:

"More green space means cooler neighborhoods, cleaner air, and healthier people. Cities with more trees spend less on healthcare and energy. We invest once—and we save for years."

She ended with a call to action:

"Let's plant the future. Not just talk about it. Let's build a city where everyone can breathe."

The room burst into applause.

Later that night, Ava watched clips of famous speeches online: Lincoln at Gettysburg. Martin Luther King Jr. on the steps of the Lincoln Memorial. Malala Yousafzai at the UN, demanding education for girls.

Each speech was different. Some were poetic. Some were simple. But all of them shared the same tools: **structure, evidence, and courage**.

That's when Ava realized something:
Great speeches aren't just about what you say. They're about **why** you say it—and **how** you make people believe.

🗣 Build a Powerful Speech: Student Structure Guide

Title of Your Speech: _____

Topic or Issue: _____

◆ 1. Hook the Audience

Start with a question, fact, quote, or story that grabs attention.

Examples:
– "Did you know our city has fewer trees per person than almost any other in the country?"
– "When my grandmother fell on a broken sidewalk, I knew something had to change."

Your Hook:

◆ 2. Present Your Claim (Main Argument)

What do you believe? What needs to change?

Example:
– "We must increase public funding for safe, green parks."

Your Claim:

◆ 3. Use Evidence and Data

Support your claim with facts, statistics, or real-world examples.

Example:
– "According to the National Health Report, neighborhoods with more green space have 20% lower asthma rates."

Your Evidence:

_____
_____
_____

◆ 4. Connect with Emotion

Tell a personal story or describe how the issue affects real people.

Example:
– "My younger brother can't safely play outside because there's no park within walking distance."

Your Story or Connection:

_____
_____
_____

◆ 5. Offer a Solution

What do you want your audience to do? Think? Change? Support?

Example:
– "Let's pass the proposal for the new Riverside Park and fund it through the Green City Grant."

Your Solution or Call to Action:

_____
_____
_____

◆ 6. Finish Strong

End with a bold statement, a hopeful vision, or a memorable quote.

Example:
– "Let's not wait. Let's grow something that lasts."

Your Closing Line:

_____

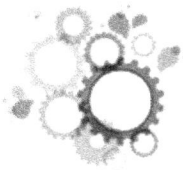

5E Lesson Plan: The STEM Behind the Speeches – Analyzing Rhetoric, Statistics & Strategy

Engage

Prompt:
Play an excerpt from a famous speech (e.g., Dr. Martin Luther King Jr., Greta Thunberg, FDR, or Emma Watson's UN speech on equality). Ask:

- What moved you in this speech?
- What statistics or facts stood out?

Explore

Activity:
Students choose a historical or modern speech that includes some use of data, science, or statistics. Examples:

- MLK's "I Have a Dream"
- JFK's Moon Speech
- Greta Thunberg's Climate Address
- Lincoln's Gettysburg Address
- Malala's UN Speech
- Sojourner Truth's "Ain't I a Woman?"

Task:

- Identify any statistics or factual claims
- Map the logical flow of the argument
- Annotate emotional, logical, and ethical appeals (pathos, logos, ethos)

Explain

Mini-Lesson Topics:

- How do facts support emotional appeals?
- What makes a claim credible?
- How can we measure the persuasive impact of a speech?

Extend

Project Options:

- Create a "STEM speech" about a social issue using data and persuasion
- Model the speech structure using flowcharts or rhetorical graphs
- Write and deliver a mini-speech using balanced persuasive strategies

STEM Focus:
Data-supported reasoning, communication modeling, impact analysis

---

Evaluate

Assessment Options:

- Annotated speech breakdown
- Speech structure graphic organizer
- Original persuasive speech using STEM support
- Reflection: What makes a speaker powerful—and responsible?

Rubric: The STEM Behind the Speeches – Analyzing Rhetoric, Statistics & Strategy

Grades 6–12 Rubric with Point Values (Total: 24 points)

Criteria	4 pts (Excellent)	3 pts (Proficient)	2 pts (Developing)	1 pt (Needs Improvement)
Speech Analysis	Accurately identifies key rhetorical strategies and data usage	Mostly accurate with minor errors	Basic analysis with some misunderstanding	Little or no accurate analysis
Data Interpretation	Clear identification and explanation of data/statistics in the speech	Basic understanding shown	Minimal effort or unclear interpretation	No reference to data or statistics
Argument Mapping	Logical flow clearly mapped with connections between claims and support	Mostly logical with some gaps	Somewhat disorganized	Unclear or missing argument structure
Creative Project (Optional Speech or Visual)	Innovative and insightful use of STEM in persuasive communication	Clear use of some STEM strategies	Basic or undeveloped concept	Missing or off-topic
Presentation & Design	Well-organized, engaging, and polished visual or speech	Mostly clear and complete	Some disorganization or confusion	Difficult to follow or incomplete
Reflection & Insight	Thoughtful reflection on power and responsibility of communication	Some reflective thinking evident	Basic summary with limited insight	Little or no reflection

Scoring Guide:

22–24: Excellent

18–21: Proficient

14–17: Developing

Below 14: Needs Improvement

Teacher Comments:

Student Reflection: What made this speech powerful? How did logic, emotion, and data work together to create impact?

Simplified Rubric (Grades 3–5)

Total Possible: 12 points

Category	3 pts – Great Job	2 pts – Getting There	1 pt – Needs Work
Speech Clarity	Understood what the speech was about	Some of the ideas are clear	Hard to understand
Facts or Data	Found and explained a number or fact	Some facts explained	No facts or unclear
Message & Voice	Speech or writing is thoughtful and creative	Some thought put into it	Unclear or rushed
Neatness & Effort	Work is neat and complete	Somewhat rushed	Messy or missing parts

Scoring Guide:

11–12: Great Job!

8–10: Keep Going!

4–7: Let's Improve It!

Student Handouts: The STEM Behind the Speeches

Introduction:

Great speeches don't just use emotion—they use logic, data, and structure to persuade. In this activity, you'll analyze how famous speeches use facts and strategy to move people and change the world.

Your Task:

1. Choose a speech from the list or find your own.

2. Identify persuasive techniques: logic, emotion, ethics (logos, pathos, ethos).

3. Highlight any use of data, statistics, or factual claims.

4. Create a visual model or graphic organizer showing how the speech is structured.

5. Optional: Write your own short speech using the same strategies.

Speech Options:

- Dr. Martin Luther King Jr. – "I Have a Dream"

- John F. Kennedy – "We choose to go to the Moon"

- Greta Thunberg – UN Climate Speech (2019)

- Sojourner Truth – "Ain't I a Woman?"

- Abraham Lincoln – Gettysburg Address

- Malala Yousafzai – UN Youth Assembly Speech

- Emma Watson – HeForShe UN Speech

Speech Analysis Table:

Section/Quote	Type of Appeal (Logos, Pathos, Ethos)	Use of Data or Facts?	Impact or Purpose

Speech Structure Visual:

Create a diagram or flowchart showing how the speech moves from:

Use arrows, boxes, or symbols to show how logic and emotion are balanced.

- Opening statement

- Key points and evidence

- Emotional high points

- Closing and call to action

Optional – Create Your Own Mini-Speech:

Use the strategies you've studied to write a short speech about a topic you care about.

Include:

- 1 statistic or fact

- 1 emotional appeal

- A clear message and call to action

Reflection Questions:

1. What was the most persuasive part of the speech you studied?

2. How did the speaker use logic and emotion together?

3. Why is it important for public communication to be both powerful and responsible?

Lesson 11: Crisis by the Numbers – Interpreting Historical Data & Decision Making

$\sim$ "The Graph in the Attic"

A Story to Introduce Decision-Making in Crisis Through Data

It was supposed to be just another boring box of old books.

But when Sam opened the dusty crate in their grandmother's attic, something strange caught their eye—a hand-drawn graph, rolled and yellowed, with jagged lines climbing and falling like a roller coaster.

"What's this?" Sam asked, holding it up.

Their grandmother took one look and smiled gently. "That," she said, "is how your great-great-grandfather saved his entire town."

Now Sam was listening.

Back in 1918, during the flu pandemic, Sam's ancestor had worked at the town post office. But he was also a numbers guy—quiet, curious, and always carrying a notebook.

"When people started getting sick," Grandma explained, "he did what he knew best: he counted."

He made daily lists of new flu cases. Tracked which neighborhoods were hit hardest. Charted hospital beds, medicine stock, even how long it took families to recover.

At first, no one paid attention. But soon, the mayor came knocking. "We don't know what's happening," he said. "Can you help?"

Sam's great-great-grandfather spread out his graphs and pointed: "If we close the school for two weeks now, we'll avoid a surge later. If we ration medicine here, more people get treated faster."

Some people called him a genius. Others said he was paranoid. But the numbers didn't lie—and the decisions made from those charts saved lives.

Sam looked closer at the old graph. Each dot was a day. Each line was a choice. "It's like reading the past in a secret code," they whispered.

Grandma nodded. "Crises aren't just chaos. They're choices. Made with the best—and sometimes the worst—information we have."

At school the next day, Sam's class began a new unit on historical crises. They compared data from the Great Depression, the Dust Bowl, and the COVID-19 pandemic.

But Sam had something special to share.

They held up the graph from the attic and said, "This is what one person with numbers can do. It might not look like much—but it changed everything."

🔢 Crisis by the Numbers: Modeling Decisions in Historical Crises

Objective:

Students will analyze real or simulated data from a historical crisis and model different decision-making scenarios. They'll explore how early action, delay, or misinformation can affect outcomes over time.

Step 1: Choose Your Crisis

Pick one of the following (or assign different ones to student groups):

1918 Flu Pandemic

The Dust Bowl

The Great Depression

COVID-19 Pandemic

Step 2: Explore the Data

Provide students with a simplified data set for their crisis, such as:

Number of cases/jobs lost/crops failed over time

Timeline of government actions or public behavior

Maps or graphs showing regional impact

Example for 1918 Flu:

Week New Cases Schools Open? Gatherings Allowed? Hospital Beds Left

Week	New Cases	Schools Open?	Gatherings Allowed?	Hospital Beds Left
1	50	Yes	Yes	100
2	150	Yes	Yes	50
3	300	No	No	30

Step 3: Model the Impact

Students create a graph or chart to model what would happen under different decision scenarios:

- What if action had been taken earlier?
- What if restrictions were lifted too soon?
- What if more resources were added halfway through?

Encourage students to track:

The number of people affected

Time to recovery

Long-term impact (economy, health, morale)

Step 4: Make a Recommendation

Each group presents:

Their modeled outcomes

The decisions that led to better (or worse) results

What they learned about data-driven leadership

Reflection Questions

How did timing change the impact of the crisis?

What role did access to information (or misinformation) play?

What does this teach us about how to prepare for future challenges?

Lesson 11: Crisis by the Numbers – Interpreting Historical Data & Decision Making

Topic: How data has shaped responses to historical crises such as wars, pandemics, economic crashes, and natural disasters

STEM Focus: Data visualization, risk modeling, statistics, systems thinking

Subjects: U.S. History, World History, Civics, Government, Math

---

💙 Teacher Letter

Dear Educator,

History is not just a story of events—it's a record of choices made in the face of uncertainty. This lesson helps students explore how leaders and communities used data to respond to crises, and how those choices impacted outcomes.

Students work with real historical statistics from events like the Great Depression, the 1918 Flu, the Dust Bowl, and the COVID-19 pandemic. They analyze trends, identify decision points, and use modeling to evaluate how information influenced policy and public behavior.

By connecting STEM tools with historical inquiry, students sharpen their ability to think critically, analyze risk, and consider the human impact of data-driven decisions.

In learning how past societies responded to crisis, students are better equipped to interpret the present—and shape the future.

With resolve and reflection,
Beverly Simmons
Author, Educator, Curriculum Developer

5E Lesson Plan: Crisis by the Numbers – Interpreting Historical Data & Decision Making

Engage

Prompt:
Display graphs showing spikes in unemployment (1930s), death tolls (1918 Flu), or food scarcity (Dust Bowl). Ask:

- What patterns do you see?
- What might cause this kind of data to change quickly?

Explore

Activity:
Students select a historical crisis to investigate. Possible topics include:

- The Great Depression (unemployment rates, bank failures)
- 1918 Influenza Pandemic (infection and death rates)
- World War II (mobilization data, rationing, production)
- The Dust Bowl (migration data, crop failures, climate)
- COVID-19 Pandemic (U.S. or global cases, school closures, equity gaps)
- Hurricane Katrina (evacuation rates, infrastructure damage)

Task:

- Gather or interpret visual data (graphs, charts, maps)
- Identify key moments where data influenced decisions
- Model outcomes with a "What if?" scenario using statistics

Explain

Discussion Topics:

- What kind of data was available at the time?
- How did leaders use it—or ignore it?
- What limitations affected decision-making?

Extend

Project Options:

- Create a timeline or infographic of crisis response with embedded data
- Build a "risk and response" simulation using data inputs
- Write a reflection comparing one historical response to a modern issue (e.g., comparing 1918 and 2020 pandemics)

STEM Focus:
Statistical reasoning, modeling, cause/effect analysis, decision impact

---

Evaluate

Assessment Options:

- Infographic or model presentation
- Data interpretation worksheet
- Written comparison of two historical events
- Reflection: "How should leaders use data during a crisis?"

Rubric: The STEM Behind the Speeches – Analyzing Rhetoric, Statistics & Strategy

Grades 6–12 Rubric with Point Values (Total: 24 points)

Criteria	4 pts (Excellent)	3 pts (Proficient)	2 pts (Developing)	1 pt (Needs Improvement)
Speech Analysis	Accurately identifies key rhetorical strategies and data usage	Mostly accurate with minor errors	Basic analysis with some misunderstanding	Little or no accurate analysis
Data Interpretation	Clear identification and explanation of data/statistics in the speech	Basic understanding shown	Minimal effort or unclear interpretation	No reference to data or statistics
Argument Mapping	Logical flow clearly mapped with connections between claims and support	Mostly logical with some gaps	Somewhat disorganized	Unclear or missing argument structure
Creative Project (Optional Speech or Visual)	Innovative and insightful use of STEM in persuasive communication	Clear use of some STEM strategies	Basic or undeveloped concept	Missing or off-topic
Presentation & Design	Well-organized, engaging, and polished visual or speech	Mostly clear and complete	Some disorganization or confusion	Difficult to follow or incomplete

Reflection & Insight	Thoughtful reflection on power and responsibility of communication	Some reflective thinking evident	Basic summary with limited insight	Little or no reflection

Scoring Guide:

22–24: Excellent

18–21: Proficient

14–17: Developing

Below 14: Needs Improvement

Teacher Comments:

Student Reflection: What made this speech powerful? How did logic, emotion, and data work together to create impact?

Simplified Rubric (Grades 3–5)

Total Possible: 12 points

Category	3 pts – Great Job	2 pts – Getting There	1 pt – Needs Work
Speech Clarity	Understood what the speech was about	Some of the ideas are clear	Hard to understand
Facts or Data	Found and explained a number or fact	Some facts explained	No facts or unclear
Message & Voice	Speech or writing is thoughtful and creative	Some thought put into it	Unclear or rushed
Neatness & Effort	Work is neat and complete	Somewhat rushed	Messy or missing parts

Scoring Guide:

11–12: Great Job!

8–10: Keep Going!

4–7: Let's Improve It!

Student Handouts: The STEM Behind the Speeches

Introduction:

Great speeches don't just use emotion—they use logic, data, and structure to persuade. In this activity, you'll analyze how famous speeches use facts and strategy to move people and change the world.

Your Task:

1. Choose a speech from the list or find your own.

2. Identify persuasive techniques: logic, emotion, ethics (logos, pathos, ethos).

3. Highlight any use of data, statistics, or factual claims.

4. Create a visual model or graphic organizer showing how the speech is structured.

5. Optional: Write your own short speech using the same strategies.

Speech Options:

- Dr. Martin Luther King Jr. – "I Have a Dream"

- John F. Kennedy – "We choose to go to the Moon"

- Greta Thunberg – UN Climate Speech (2019)

- Sojourner Truth – "Ain't I a Woman?"

- Abraham Lincoln – Gettysburg Address

- Malala Yousafzai – UN Youth Assembly Speech

- Emma Watson – HeForShe UN Speech

Speech Analysis Table:

Section/Quote	Type of Appeal (Logos, Pathos, Ethos)	Use of Data or Facts?	Impact or Purpose

Speech Structure Visual:

Create a diagram or flowchart showing how the speech moves from:

- Opening statement

- Key points and evidence

- Emotional high points

- Closing and call to action

Use arrows, boxes, or symbols to show how logic and emotion are balanced.

Optional – Create Your Own Mini-Speech:

Use the strategies you've studied to write a short speech about a topic you care about.

Include:

- 1 statistic or fact

- 1 emotional appeal

- A clear message and call to action

Reflection Questions:

1. What was the most persuasive part of the speech you studied?

2. How did the speaker use logic and emotion together?

3. Why is it important for public communication to be both powerful and responsible?

Art of STEM

Lesson 12: Innovation in Context – STEM Breakthroughs that Changed the World

·☀· "The Invention Behind the Curtain"

A Story to Introduce Innovation in Historical Context

They were cleaning out the school's basement when Eli found it.

Behind a curtain of dusty stage props and old science fair boards sat a strange contraption: a box with knobs, wires, and a crank on one side. Taped to it was a note:

"For emergencies only. Do not discard. Trust the process."

"Looks like a toaster met a typewriter," Eli joked.

Their teacher, Ms. Reyes, raised an eyebrow. "That," she said, "was our town's first emergency broadcast transmitter—built by a 12th grader in 1963."

"Wait. A student built this?" asked Eli.

"Yep. Right after a tornado destroyed half the town and nobody knew where to go. Power was out. Phones were down. So this student—Marcus Ford—built a machine that sent coded messages using Morse signals and battery-powered radios."

Eli looked at the box with new eyes. "But... why hadn't anyone invented something like this before?"

Ms. Reyes smiled. "That's what we're going to explore. Every invention has a moment. A reason. A story."

That afternoon, their class divided into teams, each investigating a different innovation: the printing press, the telegraph, the washing machine, the microchip, the solar panel. But they weren't just learning what it did—they were asking:

What *problem* did this solve?

What *resources* made it possible?

What *pressures* or *events* pushed it into reality?

Eli's group took on the telephone. They discovered how global trade made copper wire available, how rising literacy created a hunger for faster communication, and how competition between inventors shaped who got credit.

"I thought it was just a gadget," Eli said. "But it was actually about society changing—and someone noticing what people needed."

A week later, the class returned to the basement, this time with clipboards and curiosity. They studied the old transmitter, imagining what it must've felt like to invent something *because* of a crisis.

Eli ran a hand over the rusted metal. "Marcus didn't invent this in a lab. He invented it *in the moment*. That's what made it powerful."

Would you like a companion research/project sheet where students investigate an innovation in the same way Eli did? 😊

You said:

Yes please

ChatGPT said:

Here's a ready-to-use **Innovation Investigation Sheet** to pair with *"The Invention Behind the Curtain."* It guides students through analyzing not just *what* was invented—but *why, how, and what happened next*.

🧠 Innovation Investigation Sheet: Behind Every Breakthrough

Name of Innovation: _____

Inventor(s): _____

Year(s) Developed: _____

🔍 Part 1: The Problem

1. What problem or need did this invention solve?

Think about what people were struggling with or what was missing at the time.

_____

_____

2. Who was affected by the problem? Why was it important to solve?

Was it for everyday people? Industry? Government? Scientists?

_____

_____

🛠️ Part 2: The Moment

3. What was happening in history when this was invented?

Look for events, crises, trends, or social changes that influenced the timing.

_____

4. What resources (materials, skills, technology) made this invention possible?

Consider materials, energy, or knowledge that had to already exist.

⧉ Part 3: The Impact

5. How did this invention change the world—or at least the people who used it?

Think about economy, communication, safety, health, or how people lived.

---

6. What came next?

Did this innovation lead to others? Inspire more inventions? Cause unintended problems?

🎨 Part 4: Into the Future

7. If this invention were created today, how would it be different?

Would it use different tech? Be for a different audience? Solve a new version of the problem?

---

8. Can you think of a problem in today's world that might inspire a new invention?

Bonus: Sketch or describe your own "invention in the moment."

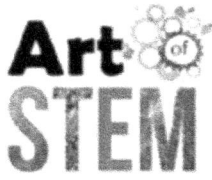

Lesson 12: Innovation in Context – STEM Breakthroughs that Changed the World

Art of STEM

Topic: Historical STEM inventions and the political, economic, and social systems that shaped their development and impact

STEM Focus: Engineering design cycle, systems thinking, cause-and-effect modeling, innovation analysis

Subjects: U.S. History, World History, Political Science, Economics, Technology

---

♥ Teacher Letter

Dear Educator,

Inventions don't happen in a vacuum. Every STEM breakthrough—from the printing press to the internet—emerged from a specific historical moment, shaped by social needs, access to resources, political priorities, and global events.

This lesson invites students to investigate a pivotal innovation and explore the systems that influenced it. Students won't just learn *what* was invented, but *why*, *how*, and *what happened next*. Through historical research, innovation modeling, and future forecasting, students will gain insight into how problem-solving connects STEM with history and civics.

By placing STEM in its real-world context, students develop a deeper understanding of how innovations evolve and how they shape—and are shaped by—society.

With curiosity and connections,
Beverly Simmons
Author, Educator, Curriculum Developer

5E Lesson Plan: Innovation in Context – STEM Breakthroughs that Changed the World

Engage

Prompt:
Show images of inventions like the printing press, steam engine, telephone, vaccine, or smartphone. Ask:

- What problem was this invention trying to solve?
- What allowed it to succeed at that moment in time?

Explore

Activity:
Students select an invention from history (or propose their own) to research. Suggested innovations:

- The Telegraph or Telephone
- The Printing Press
- Vaccination or Penicillin
- The Steam Engine
- Electricity / Lightbulb
- Internet / World Wide Web
- Artificial Intelligence
- Renewable Energy Tech (e.g., solar panels)

Task:

- Research the inventor(s), the problem it solved, and the system that made it possible (economic, political, or cultural)
- Identify unintended consequences or long-term effects
- Create a model or timeline showing the invention's context and impact

---

Explain

Mini-Lesson Topics:

- What is the engineering design cycle?
- How do STEM innovations rely on more than science (e.g., funding, timing, social readiness)?
- How can inventions shape policy or global history?

Extend

Project Options:

- Innovation Timeline: Map the path from need to invention to global impact
- Problem-Solver Forecast: What innovation does the world need now? Who could create it?
- Systems Model: Show how economy, politics, and culture affect technological success

STEM Focus:
Design thinking, systems modeling, historical cause-effect, innovation analysis

---

Evaluate

Assessment Options:

- Research summary and system model
- Timeline or infographic showing invention evolution
- Future innovation proposal with design rationale
- Reflection: "What's one invention that changed the world—and what world created it?"

Rubric: Innovation in Context – STEM Breakthroughs that Changed the World

Grades 6–12 Rubric with Point Values (Total: 24 points)

Criteria	4 pts (Excellent)	3 pts (Proficient)	2 pts (Developing)	1 pt (Needs Improvement)
Historical Research	Thorough and accurate research on invention and its context	Mostly complete with minor gaps	Basic or missing details	Little or no accurate information
Systems Thinking	Insightful explanation of how social, economic, and political systems influenced the invention	Some relevant system connections made	Limited or shallow analysis	No systems context considered
Model or Timeline	Creative, clear, and accurate visual showing invention impact	Mostly complete with relevant details	Basic or partially completed	Disorganized or off-topic
Future Thinking	Thoughtful projection of modern needs or future innovation	Somewhat original and connected to today	Limited connection to present	No future element included
Presentation & Organization	Well-organized, polished, and visually effective	Mostly clear and readable	Somewhat unclear or incomplete	Disorganized or missing elements
Reflection	Strong insight into how STEM and history interact	Basic understanding shown	Minimal insight	No reflection

Scoring Guide:

22–24: Excellent

18–21: Proficient

14–17: Developing

Below 14: Needs Improvement

Teacher Comments:

Student Reflection: How do inventions change the world—and how does the world change what we invent?

Simplified Rubric (Grades 3–5)

Total Possible: 12 points

Category	3 pts – Great Job	2 pts – Getting There	1 pt – Needs Work
Invention Facts	Explains what and who clearly	Some parts explained	Missing important parts
Why It Matters	Says how it helped the world	Some ideas shown	Not explained well
Visual or Model	Easy to understand and complete	Somewhat clear	Unclear or missing
Future Idea	Creative idea or need shown	Basic idea given	Not included

Scoring Guide:

11–12: Great Job!

8–10: Keep Going!

4–7: Let's Improve It!

Student Handouts: Innovation in Context – STEM Breakthroughs that Changed the World

Introduction:

Inventions change the world—but every invention is shaped by the world around it. In this activity, you'll research a major innovation, explore what made it possible, and think about how STEM breakthroughs are connected to social, political, and economic systems.

Your Task:

1. Choose one invention from the list or pick your own.

2. Research who invented it, why it was needed, and what happened because of it.

3. Identify the systems (like government, business, or culture) that helped or challenged the invention.

4. Make a model or timeline showing the path from idea to impact.

5. Think about what innovation the world needs next—and how it might come to life.

Innovation Choices:

- The Printing Press

- The Telegraph or Telephone

- The Steam Engine

- Penicillin or Vaccination

- The Lightbulb

- The Internet or World Wide Web

- Artificial Intelligence (past or present)

- Solar Panels or Wind Turbines

- Other STEM invention approved by your teacher

Systems Thinking Organizer:

System (Economic, Political, Cultural)	How it Helped or Blocked the Invention	Example or Evidence

Innovation Timeline or Model:

Make a diagram, flowchart, or timeline showing:

- The problem the invention solved
- Key events in its development

- Reactions from people or society
- Its long-term effects on the world

What Innovation is Needed Next?

If you could solve one global problem with STEM, what would it be?

What would your invention do?
- What systems would it depend on?

- Who would it help?
- What challenges might you face?

Reflection Questions:

1. What made your invention succeed when it did?
2. How did different systems (like government or culture) play a role?

3. How do STEM and history work together to shape the world?
4. Why is it important to think about what the world needs next?

Recap of 12 STEM-Integrated Social Studies Lessons

1. Founding a Nation – Constitution as a System

Explore the U.S. Constitution as a system of checks, balances, and decision-making. Students model government structures and simulate decision impacts.

2. Trade & Transportation – Mapping Goods, Routes & Impact

Analyze historical trade routes and transportation systems. Students map economic flows and use data to model efficiency and impact.

3. Mapping Empires – Boundaries, Power & Resistance

Use maps and historical data to investigate empires and resistance movements. Students model causes of expansion and conflict.

4. Climate, Resources & Conflict – Environmental Influence on History

Explore how geography and natural resources shaped settlements, conflict, and trade. Students interpret maps and model resource impact.

5. Data & Democracy – Voting Rights and Representation

Investigate voting rights and patterns over time. Students use data to model representation and identify inequities.

6. Data on the Move – Migration, Refugees & Global Impact

Study migration trends and their historical causes and effects. Students analyze data and map human movement across time and regions.

7. War by the Numbers – Analyzing Conflict Through Data

Examine wars through statistics on casualties, costs, and consequences. Students graph data and evaluate the true impact of war.

8. Building a Nation – Infrastructure, Innovation & Inequality

Investigate the systems behind major infrastructure projects and their impacts on equity. Students model historical access and outcomes.

9. Hidden Figures – Representation, Recognition & STEM Gaps

Highlight underrepresented figures in history and STEM. Students explore workforce data and model systems of inclusion and change.

10. The STEM Behind the Speeches – Analyzing Rhetoric, Statistics & Strategy

Dissect historical speeches with a STEM lens. Students analyze persuasive techniques, embedded data, and public messaging strategies.

11. Crisis by the Numbers – Interpreting Historical Data & Decision Making
Explore historical crises like pandemics and economic crashes through data. Students model risk, response, and decision outcomes.

12. Innovation in Context – STEM Breakthroughs that Changed the World
Research inventions and their historical context. Students model innovation paths and propose solutions for modern global problems.